VIOLENCE
IN STUDENT
WRITING

VIOLENCE

IN STUDENT
WRITING

A SCHOOL
ADMINISTRATOR'S
GUIDE

GRETCHEN OLTMAN

CORWIN
A SAGE Company

CORWIN
A SAGE Company

FOR INFORMATION:

Corwin
A SAGE Company
2455 Teller Road
Thousand Oaks, California 91320
(800) 233-9936
www.corwin.com

SAGE Publications Ltd.
1 Oliver's Yard
55 City Road
London, EC1Y 1SP
United Kingdom

SAGE Publications India Pvt. Ltd.
B 1/I 1 Mohan Cooperative Industrial Area
Mathura Road, New Delhi 110 044
India

SAGE Publications Asia-Pacific Pte. Ltd.
3 Church Street
#10–04 Samsung Hub
Singapore 049483

Acquisitions Editor: Debra Stollenwerk
Associate Editor: Desirée A. Bartlett
Editorial Assistant: Heidi Arndt
Permissions Editor: Adele Hutchinson
Project Editor: Amy Schroller
Copy Editor: Kimberly Hill
Typesetter: Hurix Systems Private Ltd.
Proofreader: Susan Schon
Indexer: Sylvia Coates
Cover Designer: Scott Van Atta

Printed in the United States of America

Library of Congress Cataloging-in-Publication Data

Oltman, Gretchen A.
Violence in student writing : a school administrator's guide / Gretchen Oltman ; foreword by Allan Osborne.

p. cm.
Includes bibliographical references and index.

ISBN 978-1-4522-0397-3 (pbk. : alk. paper)

1. School violence—United States—Prevention. 2. Violence in literature. 3. High school students' writings. 4. School management and organization—United States. I. Title.

LB3013.32.O48 2013

371.7'82—dc23

2012031311

This book is printed on acid-free paper.

SFI label applies to text stock

12 13 14 15 16 10 9 8 7 6 5 4 3 2 1

Contents

Foreword   ix
  Allan Osborne

Preface   xiii

Acknowledgments   xv

About the Author   xvii

Introduction   xix

**Chapter 1. The Aftermath of Columbine on
          Student Writing**   1

  A Brief History of School Violence   1
  The Columbine and Jonesboro Shootings:
      Writings as a Pretext for Violence   2
  The Columbine Effect   5
  The Aftermath of Columbine on the Student Writer   6
    Boston, Massachusetts   6
    Cary, Illinois   7
    West Warwick, Rhode Island   7
    Prosser, Washington   7
    Johnston, Rhode Island   7
  Summary   8
  Practical Applications for Teachers and Administrators   8
    For K–6 Schools   8
    For 7–12 Schools   9
    Questions to Consider   9

Chapter 2. Schooling for Citizenship: A Legal Primer for Educators   **11**

Freedom of Expression in Today's Public Schools   11
The U.S. Constitution   12
Tinker v. Des Moines Independent School District (1969)   13
Bethel v. Fraser (1986)   15
Hazelwood v. Kuhlmeier (1988)   16
Morse v. Frederick (2007)   18
How do these cases apply to classroom writing samples?   19
The True Threat Standard   20
The Court's Call for Citizenship Education   21
Citizenship Education Through the Curriculum   22
Courts Agree: Public Schools Are More Than
   Books and Pencils   24
Summary   26
Practical Applications for Teachers and Administrators   27
   For K–6 Schools   27
   For 7–12 Schools   28
   Questions to Consider   29

Chapter 3. School Culture and Student Safety   **31**

What Students Write About (and What It Can
   Say About Your School Culture)   32
The School Administrator's Influence on School Culture   34
Improving Your School Culture   37
Summary   38
Practical Applications for Teachers and Administrators   39
   For K–6 Schools   39
   For 7–12 Schools   40
   Questions to Consider   41

Chapter 4. Regulating Student Expression: Examining Your School Policy   **43**

Why a Zero Tolerance Approach Fails Everyone   43
Incorporating Legal Principles Into School Policies   45
Sample Policies   46
Summary   48
Practical Applications for Teachers and Administrators   48
   For K–6 Schools   48
   For 7–12 Schools   49
   Questions to Consider   50

Chapter 5. Violent Writing Within the Classroom   **51**

Freewriting Is Not the *Cause* of School Violence   52
Writing as a Predictor of Violence   54
Writing Instead of Violence   55
The Unique Nature of the Writing Classroom   56
"But, Teacher, I want to be the next Stephen King."   57
The Lost Lesson: Purpose and Audience   58
Advice for All Teachers of Writing   59
Summary   60
Practical Applications for Teachers and Administrators   61
    For K–6 Schools   61
    For 7–12 Schools   61
    Questions to Consider   62

Chapter 6. Violent Writing Beyond the Classroom   **63**

Off-Campus Writings   63
    Cases Where Schools Prevailed   64
    Cases Where Students Prevailed   65
Cyberbullying, Texting, and Facebook Writings   66
When the Violent Writing Targets You   67
Staying Informed   68
Summary   69
Practical Applications for Teachers and Administrators   70
    For K–6 Schools   70
    For 7–12 Schools   70
    Questions to Consider   71

Chapter 7. Communicating With Teachers About Violence in Student Writing   **73**

Conversing With Teachers Before the School Year Begins   73
Recognizing Potential Syllabus Problems   75
Reviewing Teacher Classroom Policies   75
Suggesting Teaching Methods When You Are
    Not a Writing Teacher   76
Continuing the Conversation   77
Summary   77
Practical Applications for Teachers and Administrators   78
    For K–6 Schools   78
    For 7–12 Schools   78
    Questions to Consider   79

Chapter 8. Threat Assessment for Student Violent
        Writing Incidents   **81**

    Assessment Does Not Mean Profiling   83
    Listening and Threat Assessment   85
    Keep a Copy of Student Writing   86
    A Sample Threat Assessment Form for Student
        Violent Writing Incidents   87
    Summary   89
    Practical Applications for Teachers and Administrators   89
        For K–6 Schools   89
        For 7–12 Schools   90
        Questions to Consider   91

Chapter 9. Acting and Responding to Student
        Violent Writing   **93**

    The Need for a Timely Response   93
    Responding Reasonably to All Student Violent Writing   95
    Creating a Documentation Trail   96
    Potential Administrative Responses   96
    Summary   98
    Practical Applications for Teachers and Administrators   98
        For K–6 Schools   98
        For 7–12 Schools   99
        Questions to Consider   99

Appendix   **101**

References and Further Reading   **103**

Index   **109**

Foreword

It is a Friday afternoon. As a principal your week has been busy with budgets, staff evaluations, and evening meetings. It has been a long week and you are tired but very much looking forward to a nice, quiet dinner with your spouse tonight followed by a relaxing weekend with your family. As you glance at the clock and think about heading for home as soon as the students have been dismissed, your school's writing teacher enters your office with an alarmed look on her face. She's usually a very calm person so you know something is up.

The writing teacher is holding a sheaf of papers. She explains that she gave an assignment to her students to write a screenplay for a short video. She hands you the papers and at the same time begins to summarize their contents. Apparently one student, known to be creative but somewhat of a loner, wrote a script about a student who felt he had been ignored and ostracized by his teachers and class-mates. The protagonist in the student's scenario gets even by plant-ing bombs in the lockers and desks of those he feels have treated him badly. The screenplay is imaginative but at the same time graphic in its detail and has an overall angry tone. The author has never been a problem student but is one who is known to guidance personnel.

Somehow you know your weekend is not going to go as planned.

While educators must take all threats to school safety seriously, at the same time we do not want to overreact or stifle creativity. Further, it cannot be overemphasized that we cannot curtail students' rights of free expression without having substantial justification. We must rec-ognize that immature students do not always understand where the line is drawn between creative expression that may have violent over-tones and expression that can be interpreted as conveying a violent intent. Most adults today clearly understand that telling a TSA agent that you have a bomb in your suitcase would never be taken as a joke. However, as recent court cases involving students being disciplined for cyberspeech indicate, students may think it is funny to post messages on social networking sites suggesting that an unpopular teacher should die. While this certainly is not acceptable behavior, it may not be anything more than a poor attempt at humor. The task for educators is to accurately identify and interpret warning signs of impending violence. In other words, they need to be able to ascertain what constitutes a true threat.

Discipline is not the primary issue here, however. Rather, it is more important to prevent an incident than to react to one that has occurred. While legal principles and definitions provide a helpful starting point, they do not give educators the guidance they need to truly interpret student expression in terms of whether it is a warning sign for impending disaster. We are all well aware that children are exposed to violence every day in the form of television shows, music, movies, video games, and even books geared specifically to young readers. While we may abhor this increase in children's exposure to violence via the media, it is a reality. Is it any wonder that violence may be a theme in students' creative writing?

As Oltman explains in her preface, there is a difference between violent writing that may be an indicator of impending action and creative writing that uses violence as a theme. School officials must take both forms of writing seriously. If the student is giving a signal, as many perpetrators have done, school personnel must take immediate action. Equally as important, if the writing provides hints of emotional or psychological distress, the school's staff also must respond by providing appropriate interventions. On the other hand, you don't want to sound a false alarm. The task for writing teachers and school administrators is to be able to tell the difference between harmless writing that expresses a violent theme and writing that expresses the violent feelings or intent of the student author. In other words, school staff must ascertain whether a student's writing constitutes a true threat. That, of course, is easier said than done.

In the scenario at the beginning of this foreword, the principal and writing teacher need to determine whether the student's writing is a signal of an impending catastrophic event or just a piece of fiction the student composed to complete the assignment. Since the student is a loner, perhaps he is angry at his peers for rejecting him and also blames his teachers for not doing something about it. On the other hand, the young writer is likely aware of what has happened throughout the country on school and college campuses and might think that such an event would be a fitting subject for the screenplay he was assigned to write. How do you know? This book will provide answers.

School administrators cannot wait until they are faced with a scenario such as the one that opens this forward. They need to anticipate that something like this may occur and be ready to respond. Such writing cannot be ignored but must be analyzed. Oltman recognizes that the task is difficult and does not profess to have all the answers. There is a fine line between writing that may include violent undertones and writing that is indicative of a disturbed mind. This book provides much guidance for school personnel in identifying the latter. After reading this book, educators will be able to detect the warning signs.

Oltman is well aware of the importance of the intersection of law, school policy, and school climate when it comes to school safety and the daily operation of educational institutions. Accordingly, she provides excellent background information on the legal issues involved in any attempts to censor student writing when issues of safety or school disruption are involved. Recognizing that prevention is the key, Oltman also discusses school climate and school policies and how these may set the stage for any interventions that may be needed down the road.

As Oltman points out, student writing is no longer confined to the classroom or publications such as the school newspaper. In the age of technology, students are able to post messages in various form on the Internet. Where once students may have left brief comments about administrators and teachers on the restroom walls, they now routinely express their negative feelings on social networking sites or discussion groups on the Web where they can be viewed by a much larger audience. This creates a legal problem regarding the extent to which school administrators may discipline students for speech created off campus (see, e.g., Osborne & Russo, in press). Oltman provides a number of guidelines for administrators and teachers who are the targets of Internet postings by students. She stresses the importance of knowing when and how to act but also knowing when it is best to ignore some comments. There have been some situations documented in court opinions where a disruption to the school was created, not by the posting but rather by an administrator's response to the comments.

Oltman provides a much-needed road map for proactively addressing violent writing. She offers sound recommendations for both classroom and schoolwide policies as well as strategies for dealing with violent writing when it occurs. One of the strengths of this book is that each chapter includes a bulleted list of recommendations for administrators and teachers at both the elementary and secondary levels. She also ends each chapter with a few thought-provoking questions to help readers evaluate their current practices and, just as important, develop new ones. These questions could easily be incorporated into professional development sessions in which educators are working on better practices to address violent writing by students.

No book can provide all the answers and no book can provide a method of addressing a problem that is right for all schools. Oltman does not try to do either. Instead she offers a protocol that schools can use to create policies, develop procedures, and assess student writing for possible risks. If you are concerned about violent expression in student writing, and you should be, this volume belongs on your bookshelf. You may read it through once, but you will refer to it often.

Allan G. Osborne Jr., EdD
Principal (Retired)
Snug Harbor Community School
Quincy, MA

Preface

Student violent writing affects every school administrator, from the elementary principal seeking to foster a creative writing environment to the senior high principal expelling a student for a graphic tale. Public school administrators are facing a unique legal obstacle in today's schools: preventing school violence and encouraging creativity. Schools aim to produce creative thinkers, artists, and writers who can become the next Maya Angelou or Steve Jobs, yet administrators often have a knee-jerk reaction to immediately suppress and discipline dark, graphic student writing, even writing that a student acknowledges is fiction. Administrators dealing with student violent writing must weigh many questions: Is the writing truly threatening? Is the writing fictional? What if a student is simply venting on paper? What guidelines should a school have in place to deal with violent student writing? What is violent student writing? And how do I know if the student behind the writing is truly violent?

Purpose of This Text

The aim of this text is to provide a solid background to this issue, from an educational, philosophical, and legal standpoint. The writing discussed in this text is *student* violent writing, not to be confused with *violent student* writing—the former being a dark, gruesome, or gory expression by an otherwise harmless student, the latter being the writings of truly disturbed and dangerous individuals. Either is bound to emerge in any school across the nation and sometimes it will be difficult to distinguish between the two. The student writings in these chapters come from several sources, some from within transcripts of published court cases, some rewritten from anecdotes shared by practicing school administrators, and some recreated from my experiences as a high school English teacher. All student identities have been protected.

Practical Uses for This Text

Each chapter ends in a concise summary in addition to a list of practical suggestions for school administrators at every level. These questions are ideal not only for practicing school administrators but also college students in teacher preparation programs, graduate students in princi-palship education programs, and practicing teachers in professional learning teams. The book is designed with informative content in the chapters and practical suggestions for implementation of the book's overall ideas. In addition, there are thought-provoking questions for educators to consider about their own practices within their own schools. In these chapters you will find the information you need to become well-versed on how to handle student violent writing in your school while protecting the integrity of student constitutional rights.

Who Should Read This Book?

If you are a school administrator, college professor, teacher, staff mem-ber, volunteer, parent, or concerned community member, you need to read this book. It is simply naïve to say "that would never happen in *my* school." There is a misconception that student violent writing only occurs in high schools or in urban communities (definitely *not* the ones that *we* live in), but violence is pervasive in every school: K–12, urban or rural, big or small. Students today are exposed to violence on TV, in their homes, and on the Internet and, in turn, they are writing about it, from the third grader drawing a gun pointed at a classmate to a group of high schoolers detailing plans about ways to kill a teacher. Each chapter in this book includes practical applications for K–6 and 7–12 schools as well as some questions for each educator to individually and thoughtfully consider. No one is immune. If you care about your safety and that of your students and children, read this book.

Three Reasons You Must Read This Text

1. You care about student safety.

2. You are committed to providing a Constitutionally-sound education.

3. You care about the overall character development of the youth in your home, your school, and your community.

Acknowledgments

I appreciate the many people who have supported this project from its inception to its conclusion. Key to the development of this topic was Dr. Donald Uerling, an outstanding advisor, mentor, and professor. He remains one of the greatest legal minds I have ever known and it has been an honor to learn with him. I am also deeply indebted to the other education professors who spent many years with me in doctoral studies, including Dr. Marilyn Grady, Dr. Larry Dlugosh, the late Dr. John Lammel, Dr. Karl Hostetler, and Professor John Gradwohl. Thanks to my teacher colleagues—particularly Dr. Mary Pflanz, Shelly Dowding, J. J. Dugdale, Kristi Leibhart, Dr. Anne Cognard, and the Lincoln East English Department for your unwavering belief in the need for this text to be in educators' hands. I owe special appreciation to my own high school creative writing teacher, Ms. Deborah McGinn, who allowed me to experience freedom through writing. I am also grateful to my husband, Ron, and my parents, Ron and Phyllis Hall, who have supported my passion and devotion to educating teachers and administrators about this topic. I am fortunate to have married into a family made up of a multitude of educators who have invested their lives wholeheartedly in education—and I am so thankful to the Oltmans for their love and enthusiasm. A big thank you to Dr. Allan Osborne for his thoughtful foreword and supportive attitude toward this text. Much appreciation goes to Debra Stollenwerk for taking the time to pursue this text and believing in me as an author, to Kimberly Greenberg for her diligent assistance in the preparation of this text, and to Kimberly Hill for her exceptional editing skills. A special thanks goes to Kevin and Liz Henning, owners of the Kava House Cafe in Crete, Nebraska, who created an encouraging writing environment while also running a business. Thank you for the endless cups of hot cocoa and supportive words along the way.

I dedicate this book to my children, Amy and Bryce, and to the many teachers and administrators who have shared their stories with me.

Publisher's Acknowledgments

Corwin gratefully acknowledges the contributions of the following reviewers:

Susan N. Imamura, Principal (Retired)
Manoa Elementary School, Honolulu, HI

Robin E. Ruiz, Teacher
Denison Middle School, Winter Haven, FL

Marilyn Steneken, Science Teacher
Sparta Middle School, Oak Ridge, NJ

Kelly VanLaeken, Principal
Ruben A. Cirillo High School, Walworth, NY

Marian White-Hood, Director of Academics
Maya Angelou Public Charter Schools, Washington, DC

About the Author

Photo by Craig Chandler.

Gretchen Oltman, JD, PhD, has spent over a decade in education, including many years as a high school English teacher. She is a licensed attorney in the state of Nebraska and holds a PhD in Educational Studies from the University of Nebraska. Oltman spent most of her career as a high school teacher focused on Freshman English courses. In addition, Oltman successfully team taught a course for struggling readers and writers, developed a new elective course called "Law and Literature," and served on building and districtwide assessment committees. She has also served as a lecturer of Education Law in the Department of Educational Administration at the University of Nebraska-Lincoln as well as a graduate program administrator at the University of Nebraska College of Law. Oltman currently works as the District Secondary Gifted Education Facilitator for Bellevue Public Schools in Bellevue, Nebraska. She was awarded the 2010 Dr. Ted Sizer High School Level Dissertation of the Year by the National Association of Secondary School Principals. She has been a presenter at national conferences for the NASSP, Education Law Association, and several local and state organizations.

Introduction

I began my high school English teaching career in the fall of 1999 at a typical Midwestern high school. The fall of 1999 was not any normal school year. It was less than six months after the tragic shootings at Columbine High School in Littleton, Colorado. Memories of the events were starting to fade but were still present in every teacher's mind. After all, the teachers at Columbine did not imagine two students sitting in their classes would return to school one April day and open fire on faculty and students before committing suicide. There was a shocking normalcy to Columbine—one that as a teacher in a neighboring state, I could somehow gruesomely imagine.

It was on a hot August day when I first encountered my Literature 100 students. This was a rough crowd of juniors and seniors. Several were on the verge of graduating and heading to college. Others were still trying to make up credit for failing their entire freshman year. Others were wearing ankle-monitoring bracelets. I was bright-eyed and enthusiastic. Having just left law school, I returned to the classroom with a renewed freshness and enthusiasm. I was going to be a *great* teacher. One of the first assignments for this crew was for each of them to write me a letter about themselves. This was an assignment I had done countless times as an English major in college and I figured it would translate well into my high school English classroom. After all, I had studied leading English methods professors—Nancie Atwell, Jim Burke, and others who promoted making personal connections with students through writing. Somewhere in my imagination I was huddled up around a cup of hot cocoa, reading these letters from students who were sharing their desires to become doctors and teachers, who were caring about their fellow students, and who really, really wanted to learn from the pages of literature we were about to encounter in my class.

The following day I hunkered down with my pile of student letters. "Dear Mrs. Oltman," one read, "My name is Stacy and I'm a senior. I work at the senior center at night. On the weekend I compete in gymnastics and swimming." Pretty innocuous stuff, useful for getting to know the hobbies and interests of my students. Most were this type of letter. I stopped when I got to this one, "Dear Mrs. Oltman. I am the worst person you'll ever meet. I can do drugs better than anyone. I like to pa-a-a-r-ty and shoot guns. I would watch out if I were you." I was not sure what to do. Was this a joke? Was it a kid who was mocking my assignment? Was this a serious threat to me? I put the note in the bottom of the pile and stuffed the stack in my backpack. Should I tell someone? Do I call his parents? Who do I tell? I did nothing.

Eventually the routine of the school year set in and Columbine became a fading memory. Students became familiar, routines were established, and friendships were formed. I still had the letters in my backpack but I never revisited that stack. Nothing happened. I was not shot, hurt, or even threatened. The school year was uneventful. Yet it was during that first year of teaching that I gained a heightened appreciation for what happened at Columbine in my own way. I ran across a New York Times article discussing the Columbine shooters and, in particular, their English teacher. This teacher had apparently received some pretty graphic writings from Klebold and Harris in her class and had notified the parents of the shooters. Klebold had written a story describing a shooting and yet was able to convince his mom and a school counselor that it was "just a story." Harris's response to a class assignment to write from the viewpoint of an inanimate object chose to write from the viewpoint of a shotgun shell. For film class, the two had created a video where they wore black trench coats, carried guns through the school hallways, and appeared to cause explosions as they made their way through the building (Brooke, 1999).

I read another article about the regret an Arkansas English teacher felt after having read a student's essay and never reporting the contents of it until after the student had shot and killed four students and one English teacher in 1998 (Heard, 1999). The student had been assigned to write an essay for English class about why he had been assigned to in-school suspension earlier in the day. The essay, written about 14 months prior to the shootings, expressed the shooter's desire to shoot "squirrels" (para. 10), referring to teachers and students he was mad at over an altercation about a hat he wanted to wear in school. Even though the writing preceded the shooting by over one year, the teacher discussed the essay and noted that English teachers should pay attention to the warning signs that arise in student writing.

I began to wonder about my own teaching and the practice of writing itself. After all, we ask students to write in all sorts of contexts all day long. Students write in journals, essays, worksheet responses, blogs, texts, and letters. The teaching practices behind the writing assignments are sound, but the responses are sometimes questionable. The models I had learned in English methods classes encouraged freethinking, free writing, the ability to express one's opinion, and to differ from the majority. But where was the line? When did asking students to write create the next potential Columbine? Could I get in trouble for my writing assignments? Who was there to help me figure it out? Was there really a problem with how I learned to teach writing and how the real world really worked?

The reality of school shootings was, at most, a newsworthy and interesting intellectual event to me until January 2010. A tragic school shooting happened within 15 miles of where I live, killing a school administrator and wounding another. The student, who had documented troubles at school, had met with his school assistant principal, Vicki Kaspar, to receive a suspension for some behavior he had engaged in over winter break. The student left the building, went to his police-officer–father's apartment, retrieved his police weapon before returning to school to fatally shoot Kaspar and wound Principal Curtis Case. I have imagined how it felt to be Kaspar, sitting at my desk in the school office and seeing this student walk into my office, shut the door, and quietly look down the barrel of his gun. You see, I live in the heartland of the United States where things like this do not happen. Yet, it did, and while this was not a situation of documented student writing leading to this particular violent event, it illustrates the magnitude of issues school administrators face today—and some of those issues are ones of life and death.

1

The Aftermath of Columbine on Student Writing

Your tragedy, though it is unique in its magnitude, is, as you know so well, not an isolated event.

—President Bill Clinton
Addressing Columbine High School, May 20, 1999

A Brief History of School Violence

Without newsworthy school violence incidents, student violent writing would probably not be as concerning to educators as it currently is. After all, for most students, school is the safest place to be during the day. School violence has been documented since around 1927 when a disgruntled taxpayer planted dynamite at a Michigan school killing 38 students, 2 teachers, the school superintendent, and the village postmaster (*USA School Violence Statistics*, n.d.). Since then, educators have seen the culmination of widely publicized school shootings such as those in Littleton, Colorado; Jonesboro, Arkansas; Virginia Tech University; and Texas A&M University.

Violence is not absent in today's schools. While the rate of serious violent crimes in public school has actually dropped over the last decade, students still face personal danger while attending school

(Department of Justice, cited in National Center for Education Statistics, 2007). In a 2003 survey, 17% of high school students had carried a weapon to school during the 30 days preceding the survey (Grunbaum et al., 2004). In 2010, the U.S. Department of Education presented a set of findings from a random school survey that nearly half of the surveyed schools reported at least one student threat of physical attack without a weapon. Thirty-nine percent of surveyed middle schools reported that student bullying occurred at school at least once a week. While the actual numbers of violent incidents or widely publicized events might be decreasing, the rate of students reporting bullying, harassment, and emotional threats has been on the increase. The U.S. Department of Education noted,

> Highly publicized school shootings have created uncertainty about the security of this country's schools and generated a fear that an attack might occur in any school, in any community. Increased national attention to the problem of school violence has prompted educators, law enforcement officials, mental health professionals, and parents to press for answers to two central questions: "Could we have known that these attacks were being planned?" and if so, "What could we have done to prevent these attacks from occurring?" (Fein et al., 2002, p. 3)

So while the overall numbers seem promising, as long as students face danger at school, educators will be questioning whether violence prevention methods are actually effective in practice.

The Columbine and Jonesboro Shootings: Writings as a Pretext for Violence

The 1999 school shooting at Columbine High School in Littleton, Colorado, left 15 people dead, 23 students wounded, and a nation of school administrators wondering "How can I prevent the same thing from happening at my school?" The images were gruesome and played out on live national TV—aerial footage of students running from the school building, hands in the air, some badly wounded, some left to die on the sidewalk surrounding the school. During that event, two students, Eric Harris and Dylan Klebold, had walked into their school dressed in trench coats and shooting anyone in their path.

Documents released by Jefferson County authorities nearly four years after the shooting provided a shocking glimpse into the writings of Harris and Klebold. Dylan Klebold was a vivid writer and journaler. He began a personal journal nearly two years before the shooting titled "Existences: A Virtual Book." He wrote often of lost love, disappointment, and suicidal tendencies. Around February 1999, Klebold wrote a short story for English class revolving around an angry man in black methodically killing "preps." He stated, "If I could face an emotion of god, it would have looked like the man. I not only saw in his face but also felt emanating from him power, complacence, closure, and godliness. The man smiled, and in that instant, through no endeavor of my own, I understood his actions" (Cullen, 2009, p. 307). The story ended with the impact of the murder on the man left behind.

This story left Klebold's English teacher in confusion as to how to approach the content of the writing. The teacher, Judy Kelly, spoke with Klebold who told her it was "just a story." Kelly then contacted Klebold's parents who noted how hard kids are to understand sometimes. Kelly then contacted the school counselor who heard a similar defense from Klebold. After the shooting occurred, a classmate of Klebold's commented on the class stating, "It's a creative writing class. You write about what you want. Shakespeare wrote all about death" (Cullen, 2009, p. 308).

Eric Harris had received positive teacher comments about his graphic violent writing. In 1997, Harris began to notice school shootings in the news and wrote a paper for English class in which he wrote, "It is just as easy to bring a loaded handgun to school as it is to bring a calculator." His teacher's response was, "Thorough and logical. Nice job." In 1999 Harris wrote an essay for English class titled "Is Murder or Breaking the Law Ever Justified?" The same year he wrote a paper for government class wherein he admitted he was a felon and how a night in jail had made him a changed man. It ended, "I guess it was a worthwhile punishment after all." The teacher responded, "Wow, what a way to learn a lesson. I agree that night was punishment enough for you. Still, I am proud of you and the way you have reacted . . . You have really learned from this and it has changed the way you think . . . I would trust you in a heartbeat. Thanks for letting me read this and for being in my class." In another class writing where Harris was to respond to a Shakespeare reading, he wrote about how he idolized a character that would not be taken without a struggle.

One document, a 13-page essay written by Klebold the fall before the shootings took place, explored Klebold's explorations into the beliefs of Charles Manson and his theory that he had the right to kill people that had corrupted the Earth and "dumped him" (Ingold & Pankratz, 2003). He also wrote about the movie *Natural Born Killers*, stating that the movie portrayed two characters that "defy society and get lost in their own little world, killing and robbing whomever they came across" (p. A-01). Eric Harris wrote a fiction piece about an alien attack that killed his Marine buddies. He used phrases such as "Bullet shells sprinkled the floor, on top of a carpet of blood," and "Arms, legs, and heads were tossed about as if a small child turned on a blender with no lid in the middle of a room" (p. A-01). While such writing was dark and violent, the part that troubled many school administrators was the positive response of the teachers who had read the writings. One teacher offered "Your paper is very good" to Klebold and "Yours is a unique approach and your writing works in a gruesome way" to Harris (p. A-01, see also Brooke, 1999).

This type of situation cannot only be found in the aftermath of the Columbine shootings. In March 1998, two middle school students in Jonesboro, Arkansas, shot and killed four students and one teacher. The boys, Mitchell Johnson and Andrew Golden, had arranged a plan wherein Golden asked to be excused from his class, pulled a fire alarm, and ran into the woods outside the school to join Johnson. While students exited the building because of the sounding fire alarm, Johnson and Golden opened fire. A 1999 newspaper article detailed the regret an English teacher felt after the Jonesboro shooting. As a result of a minor incident at school involving an altercation over a hat he was prohibited from wearing to school, one of the shooters had been assigned to write an essay for English class about why he was assigned in-school suspension for the incident. The essay, written about 14 months prior to the shootings, expressed the student's desire to shoot "squirrels," referring to teachers and students. Even though the shooting occurred over a year after the essay was written, the teacher noted her guilt about not knowing what the essay truly foretold and noted the importance for English teachers to pay attention to warning signs in student writing (Heard, 1999).

School administrators, then, were in a bind. Did these writings really foretell events about to occur at Columbine High or were the writings merely adolescent experiments in thought construction and creativity? Were all writings of a similar nature signs of impending violent acts? Is it a school's duty to start suppressing types or styles of student writing?

The Columbine Effect

School administrators could not sit idly back and ignore the content of student writings after the Columbine shootings. As a result a new term— *Columbine effect*—emerged in literature detailing the litigation spawned by the Columbine shootings. Calvert and Richards (2003) wrote:

> Quite simply, the events at Columbine gave high school administrators all the reasons—legitimate or illegitimate— they needed to trounce the First Amendment rights of public school students in the name of preventing violence. The first wave of censorship cases that swelled up in the year immediately following Columbine is now well documented. But the fear of Columbine-like violence that gave rise to that wave has not subsided in the years since. As the Washington Post observed in December 2002, many school administrators across the country "are still on edge since the tragedy at Columbine High School." (p. 1091)

Columbine was in the back of everyone's minds, including those of judges deciding the fate of student First Amendment privileges in public schools. One judge wrote about his support for a student expulsion based on the content of a student's summer writings from home wherein he described his desire to rape, sodomize, and murder a fellow classmate. After the writing was unknowingly taken from the student and found on school grounds, the judge wrote his support for the student's expulsion by stating, "we find it untenable in the wake of Columbine and Jonesboro that any reasonable school official who came into possession of J.M.'s letter would not have taken some action based on its violent and disturbing content" (*Doe v. Pulaski County Special School District*, 2002, Footnote 4, p. 626). Basically, this court was saying that it would have been irresponsible, knowing what had gone on at Columbine and Jonesboro, to not take action against the student.

Another court wrote about a student's expulsion based on the content of a website created at home. The court held that the website was an interference with the work of the school and went on to state, "We too appreciate that in schools today violence is unfortunately too common and the horrific events at Columbine High School, Colorado, remain fresh in the country's mind" (*J.S. v. Bethlehem Area School District*, 2002, p. 659). Again, an example of a court acknowledging current events—that in light of the current events, administrators had every right to be leery of the intent of student writing.

Calvert and Richards (2003) wrote an article titled, "Columbine fallout: The long-term effects on free expression take hold in public schools." The authors stated that the events at Columbine "gave high school administrators all the reasons—legitimate or illegitimate—they needed to trounce the First Amendment rights of public school students in the name of preventing violence" (p. 1090). The authors traced a growing trend of post-Columbine cases in which schools were prevailing in their attempts to suppress student expression. Reviewing cases from 2002 to 2003, the authors concluded that school administrators were frequently using the "true threat" exception to the First Amendment as the primary way of suppressing student expression. That is, administrators were eager to deem a student's expression as "threatening" in order to implement student discipline for the content of the expression. The authors noted, "Disputes that once would have been settled by a call home to parents now end up in court due to overzealous school officials who have exploited the tragedy at Columbine to squelch speech they find disagreeable" (p. 1139).

The Aftermath of Columbine on the Student Writer

As newsworthy as Columbine proved to be, so do the disciplinary tales of public school students attending school in the post-Columbine era. These events serve as specific examples of students who were often writing within the confines of the directions provided by teachers in school and were disciplined for the content of their writings. While certainly not representative of every school or every school administrator, the events are cautionary tales of how the writing landscape has changed for students in the past few years.

Boston, Massachusetts

In 2000, a high school student in Boston, Massachusetts, was suspended for his response to a class assignment to "write a horror story about a mysterious person." (Boston Schools Drop, 2000). The instructor of the course told students that no subject was off-limits. One student, Charles Carithers, wrote a story in which the main character attacked his high school English teacher with a chain saw. At the end of the story readers learn that the narrator's aunt, not the English teacher, was the person who died in the story. Carithers's English teacher reported the content of the essay to school administrators who promptly suspended him for three days.

Cary, Illinois

In 2007, an 18-year-old student was arrested in Cary, Illinois, based on the content of his writing for an English assignment. This straight-A student was basically told that no topic was off limits and students were not to judge or censor their writing process. The student wrote an essay titled "Blood, Sex, and Booze" where he insinuated his teacher could inspire one to commit a school shooting (Swedberg & Olson, 2007). The English teacher reported the issue to school administrators who then notified the police. The student was arrested and charged with two counts of disorderly conduct, which were later dropped. The student was eventually allowed to return to school but suffered losing his recruit status to the U.S. Marine Corps because of the charges filed against him (Attorney: Teen Who Wrote, 2007).

West Warwick, Rhode Island

The U.S. Secret Service investigated a seventh-grade student after he penned a classroom assignment to write about his perfect day. His "perfect day" included harming the president, Oprah, and various corporate executives. The student was interrogated by the U.S. Secret Service—quite a task for a seventh grader (Secret Service Investigates, 2006).

Prosser, Washington

A high school student was questioned by the U.S. Secret Service for drawings he completed as part of an art class assignment. The drawings included depictions of the president's head on a stick and one of the president characterized as the devil launching a missile. The art teacher turned the drawings over to the school administrators who then contacted law enforcement authorities. The student was disciplined but not suspended for his drawings (Secret Service Questions, 2004).

Johnston, Rhode Island

An 11th grade honors student was suspended indefinitely based on the content of an extra credit journal he kept for his Honors English class. The student, Matthew Parent, was instructed to use the journal to express his ideas and engage in freewriting. Parent wrote a violent piece where he wrote, "They fear I'll kill them. They know I have no limits, no remorse, and nothing to lose." The teacher turned the writings over to the school counselor, who then contacted a psychologist. The student was suspended indefinitely and was determined to be homicidal and suicidal. Legal wrangling went on and eventually the school reinstated Parent without forcing a psychological evaluation to be completed (Rhode Island School Settles, 2001).

Summary

Students across the nation are still living with the aftermath of Columbine. Judges give weight to administrators making difficult disciplinary decisions in light of the Columbine aura. My experience as a classroom teacher highlighted this problem: Teachers in all curricular areas are attempting to teach writing skills using sound methodology and students are sometimes responding with violent content. Because of heightened publicity about school violence, administrators are on guard and swift to react to violent content. However, students who face discipline for the content of their writings, as either a class assignment or random writing within the school, can sue alleging a violation of First Amendment rights. Administrators and teachers are caught in the crossfire: suppress all student violent writing in the hope of preventing school violence or allow it with the goal of creating better writers? It is not only important for school administrators to know the basic legal principles guiding student writing scenarios but also to understand the moral and philosophical reasoning presented in prominent case law as to why the content of student writing should be a primary concern within schools today.

Practical Applications for Teachers and Administrators

For K–6 Schools

- Participate in a violence prevention curriculum; this may be a one-time investment. For a lower cost, perhaps partner with your local law enforcement to form a partnership violence prevention program.
- Help students feel safe in school by having high staff visibility throughout the building at all times.
- Appoint a school counselor or other trusted staff member as a safe person to talk to about violent events students may have witnessed at home or elsewhere.

- Acknowledge that violent writing is not a high school-only problem. Address this with your staff members.
- Allow students multiple writing opportunities throughout your curriculum to practice formulating appropriate brainstorming protocol.
- Host essay contests and other positive events to reward productive, positive writing.
- Begin discussing student violent writing with parents and community members. Provide some warning signs that younger students might show in their writings.

For 7–12 Schools

- Don't obsess about school violence events when they occur or are highly publicized in the news. If possible, refrain from changing school policies or procedures that are simply a result of fear from publicized school violence events.
- Participate in school violence prevention programs or partner with your local law enforcement to provide school violence prevention curriculum.
- Create a hotline for students to anonymously report potentially violent behavior.
- Acknowledge that violent intentions are often expressed in writing. Communicate with your staff, parents, and students that all written threats or statements will be taken seriously.
- Never joke about school violence.
- Pay attention to school violence events that occur throughout the nation. Use each as a learning moment: Study the student pattern, the administrative response, and the potential implications for your school community. Discuss this with your school attorney.

Questions to Consider

1. How has school violence affected your community or school?

2. What are violence statistics in your community and within your school? How do these statistics influence how you lead your school? Who can you contact in your community or school district to learn more specifics about school violence statistics?

3. Are your teachers and staff members prepared to work with students who might face violence outside of school?

4. What inservice opportunities are available for your school faculty to learn more about working with students with violent backgrounds?

5. How do you communicate with parents and stakeholders about any violence that occurs within your school?

2

Schooling for Citizenship

A Legal Primer for Educators

That they are educating the young for citizenship is reason for scrupulous protection of constitutional freedoms of the individual, if we are not to strangle the free mind at its source and teach youth to discount important principles of our government as mere platitudes.

—West Virginia Board of Education v. Barnette (1943)

Freedom of Expression in Today's Public Schools

School administrators in today's public schools are charged with knowing a lot about the law in a variety of settings. From attendance laws to due process procedures to laws dictating teacher appraisal, it is not hard to get confused and misled by legalese and one-sided propaganda. After all, a principal is not a lawyer and yet is responsible for making multiple legally binding decisions in just one day. The area of student speech and expression is no less difficult to navigate than any other school law area. The U.S. Supreme Court has ruled on four separate student expression and speech cases in the past four decades, helping guide how school administrators can legally restrict student expression and speech so that the conduct of the school day can seamlessly occur. However, the four cases provide a lot of room for discussion and interpretation and school administrators must tread slowly and cautiously through the guidelines set forth in order to behave in a constitutional fashion.

This chapter presents a summary of the four presiding U.S. Supreme Court cases. In addition, some discussion about the "true threat" standard is outlined as it is generally the one sure way an administrator can suppress truly threatening student expression. While school administrators are not attorneys and cannot be expected to store a wealth of changing legal knowledge, they can be well versed on existing U.S. Supreme Court law and how it applies to student expression. With a limited number of cases to deal with (4), every school administrator can be familiar with common language and principles from applicable U.S. Supreme Court public school cases. Specifically, when a student produces a violent or disturbing piece of writing, school administrators can rely on existing U.S. Supreme Court law to guide disciplinary strategies. Being familiar with these principles makes it easier for school administrators to understand the confines and principles supported and denounced by the land's highest court.

The U.S. Constitution

The First Amendment of the U.S. Constitution states, "Congress shall make no law . . . abridging the freedom of speech, or of the press, or the right of the people peaceably to assemble." The Fourteenth Amendment makes these principles applicable to state government actors, such as public schools and school administrators, as well. In constitutional cases, plaintiffs often sue school districts under a Federal statute as well, section 1983 of title 42 of the U.S. Code (2000), which was enacted as part of the Civil Rights Act of 1871:

> Every person who, under color of any statute, ordinance, regulation, custom, or usage, of any State or Territory or the District of Columbia, subjects, or causes to be subjected, any citizen of the United States or other person within the jurisdiction thereof to the deprivation of any rights, privileges, or immunities secured by the Constitution and laws, shall be liable to the party injured in an action at law, suit in equity, or other proper proceeding for redress, except that in any action brought against a judicial officer for an act or omission taken in such officer's judicial capacity, injunctive relief shall not be

granted unless a declaratory decree was violated or declaratory relief was unavailable. For the purposes of this section, any Act of Congress applicable exclusively to the District of Columbia shall be considered to be a statute of the District of Columbia.

These three pieces of legislation combined—the U.S. Constitution's First and Fourteenth Amendments and the Civil Rights Act—give students the ability to challenge disciplinary action or suppression of student expression that exceeds the powers given to government officials. While this sounds complicated and daunting, the application of these primary sources within the nation's public schools are limited to four reigning U.S. Supreme Court cases, which are limited in scope and applicability depending on the facts that arise during the school day.

Tinker v. Des Moines Independent School District (1969)

Tinker v. Des Moines Independent School District (1969) was the first U.S. Supreme Court case dealing with regulation of student expression. In 1965, during the height of war protests and student demonstrations across the nation, three students wore black armbands to school to protest United States involvement in the Vietnam War. The three students, a 13-year-old girl, her 15-year-old brother, and a 16-year-old friend, planned to wear the black armbands in conjunction with fasting during the winter holiday season in protest of the political controversy. When the school learned of the students' intent to wear the armbands, the principals quickly passed a "no-armband" rule providing that a student wearing an armband to school would be asked to remove it and if the student refused, he or she would be suspended until he or she removed the armband. In this school setting, students were permitted to wear other controversial symbols, including political campaign buttons and even the Iron Cross, a traditional symbol for Nazism—simply not black armbands. Shortly after the rule was implemented, the three wore the armbands to school. The armband-clad students were suspended until they agreed to return to school without the armbands. They did not return to school until after the planned holiday period of protest had ended, after the New Year's holiday. The students' parents (on behalf of the students) filed suit in federal court against school officials seeking an injunction from imposition of the discipline. A lower court sided with the school, stating that school officials were justified in fearing the armbands would cause a disruption. The students appealed the lower court's support of the school, and the case eventually wound its way to review by the U.S. Supreme Court. The U.S. Supreme Court stated that students do not "shed their constitutional rights to freedom of speech or expression at the schoolhouse gate" and held that the school officials had acted inappropriately (p. 505). The court focused on the purposes of the public school stating, "In our system, state-operated schools may not be enclaves of totalitarianism. School officials do not possess absolute authority over their students," (p. 511) and "In our system, students may not be regarded as closed-circuit recipients of only that which the State chooses to communicate" (p. 511). They also stated, "Our history says that it is this sort of hazardous freedom—this kind of openness—that is the basis of our national strength and of the independence and vigor of Americans who grow up and live in this relatively permissive, often disputatious, society" (p. 508). The court did write that under different circumstances school officials may have acted appropriately and thus created the *Tinker* standard. The standard set forth by the U.S. Supreme Court regarding suppressing expression articulates that if a school authority can reasonably forecast "substantial disruption or material interference with school activities" then they may suppress student expression at school (p. 514). Had, for instance, there been student arguments in classrooms about the Vietnam War or fights taking place on school grounds relating to war protests, then school administrators could have made an argument that the potential for a disruption was so likely the armbands simply could not be tolerated on campus. However, the administrators did not document any indication of substantial disruption or material interference to the school day. Instead, it appeared the administrators were simply looking to avoid an uncomfortable situation by preempting the wearing of the armbands. In this instance, quiet protest by the students did not rise to the level of a substantial disruption or material interference with school activities. The court noted that expression that "materially disrupts class work or involves substantial disorder or invasion of the rights of others" is not constitutionally protected. In other words, if a teacher is unable to teach or students are unable to learn because of the disruption caused by the expression, then a school administrator is acting appropriately by suppressing the expression.

Tinker is an important case for school administrators in that it is the first case dealing specifically with student expression in public schools and is the foundation for all later cases. It was a strong statement by the court that school administrators cannot suppress student expression simply because they do not like it or it is uncomfortable to hear or read. The court set forth a relatively high standard for administrators to meet—that administrators must be able to document an impending disruption or interference to the school day and only then can they move forward to suppress student expression. When a student writes something violent, administrators cannot simply expel the student because of the message itself but must carefully weigh the standards set forth in *Tinker* to determine if the writing caused or could cause a substantial disruption or material interference. If the writing does not rise to this level of disruptiveness, an administrator must find an alternative way of dealing with the writing other than outright suppression.

Bethel v. Fraser (1986)

The next student speech case to reach the U.S. Supreme Court was *Bethel School District No. 403 v. Fraser* (1986), which involved a speech at a student assembly about self-government. Matthew Fraser, a high school junior, was helping a friend run for a student government office. In a speech nominating his friend, Fraser used numerous sexual innuendo and references. Before presenting his speech, Fraser consulted two teachers and both teachers warned him not to give the speech. During the speech some students "hooted and yelled; some by gestures graphically simulated the sexual activities pointedly alluded to in the respondent's (Fraser) speech" (p. 678). The day after the speech, Fraser was called into the assistant principal's office and told he was being suspended for three days because he violated the school's "disruptive-conduct" rule, which stated, "Conduct which materially and substantially interferes with the educational process is prohibited, including the use of obscene, profane language or gestures." Fraser's name was also removed from a list of potential graduation speakers. Fraser appealed the school administrator's decision through the school district's grievance procedures, where the hearing officer upheld the discipline imposed by the school administrator. Fraser served two days of his suspension and returned to school on the third day. Fraser (through his father) filed suit against the school district, claiming the school district violated his First Amendment rights and seeking an injunction and monetary relief. The U.S. District Court that initially heard the case agreed with Fraser and held that the school's sanction against Fraser violated his First Amendment rights. On appeal, the Ninth Circuit Court of Appeals similarly agreed that the school had overstepped its bounds by disciplining Fraser for the speech. Finally, the U.S. Supreme Court reversed the Ninth Circuit Court of Appeals's decision in favor of Fraser's stance, stating that "the undoubted freedom to advocate unpopular and controversial views in schools and classrooms must be balanced against the society's countervailing interest in teaching students the boundaries of socially appropriate behavior" (p. 681). The court found that Fraser's speech, given in the context of the public school setting, was inappropriate and that the school had the authority to discipline Fraser for its content. The court stated, "it is a highly appropriate function of public school education to prohibit the use of vulgar and offensive terms in public discourse" (p. 683). In addition, the court wrote that the students in the audience were essentially captive, and thus, the school had a right to limit the messages being presented. The court stated that allowing Fraser to give the speech would have undermined the school's educational mission. Last, the court also noted that public school students do have First Amendment rights, but those rights are not the same as adults in other settings. As a result, student speech that is vulgar, lewd, or plainly offensive may be regulated by public schools.

Fraser is an important case for school administrators dealing with student violent writing in that it presents a situation where a student said something vulgar in front of an audience of his peers and the school administration's discipline of him was upheld. This case gives the school administrator latitude to act swiftly if student expression is vulgar, lewd, or plainly offensive. In addition, the court also presented some discussion that supported the need for schools to have some latitude to actually function during the day and not simply stand by when student expression disrupts the basic educational mission of the school day. Therefore, if an administrator can show that a piece of student writing undermined the school's educational mission or that it was vulgar, lewd, and or plainly offensive, student discipline for the content of the writing is quite easy.

Hazelwood v. Kuhlmeier (1988)

The next student expression case the Supreme Court decided was in 1988. *Hazelwood School District v. Kuhlmeier* (1988) is widely known for permitting administrative censorship for school-sponsored publications, such as student newspapers or yearbooks. The newspaper involved in *Hazelwood* was part of the curriculum in the school's journalism class. As students prepared to put the newspaper to press, the school principal notified them that they would need to remove two articles. One article involved teen pregnancy, and the other involved a discussion of the impact of divorce on teenagers. The issue was not that the principal outright disagreed or disapproved of the edition's content but that some of the content was sensitive and needed more time to be edited. The principal thought that information in the articles was inappropriate for the newspaper and there simply was not enough time to change the content before the end of the school year. Therefore, he asked that the questionable material be completely removed from the paper. The students objected and filed suit, claiming their First Amendment rights had been violated by the school principal. The U.S. Supreme Court found that the school principal had properly exercised his discretion and held that "educators do not offend the First Amendment by exercising editorial control over the style and content of student speech in school-sponsored expressive activities so long as their actions are reasonably related to legitimate pedagogical concerns" (p. 273). The newspaper in this case, bearing the school's name, would appear to endorse the articles within and this, the court reasoned, provided a legitimate rationale for the school to monitor its contents. The court ruled that the school did not create a public forum through its issuance of the newspaper and did indeed have editorial control over the publication. The court also presented justification for a school to restrict curricular speech. It allowed the school administrator to restrict student speech so that "[1] participants learn whatever lesson the activity is designed to teach, [2] that readers or listeners are not exposed to material that may be inappropriate for their level of maturity, and [3] that the views of the individual speaker are not erroneously attributed to the school" (p. 271). Therefore, the school may regulate school-sponsored student speech as long as the school has legitimate pedagogical concerns behind its restrictions.

Hazelwood, while often considered the "school newspaper" case, supports the notion that schools have curricular goals and are not simply acting haphazardly through content areas. Teaching students how to write for an appropriate audience, helping students gauge professional writing standards, and even helping students understand the writing process itself are all pedagogical concerns that would support suppressing student expression under *Hazelwood*. When dealing with student violent expression, this idea can become quite muddy because when an English assignment is made, a violent response is often not anticipated. However, if an administrator can show that suppressing the student writing is necessary to support the curricular goals (teaching the writing process, having students learn how to write for an appropriate audience) the argument for suppression of the writing becomes somewhat less troublesome. Administrators should consider the overall goals of the curriculum when faced with a piece of student violent writing and should ask if there is a curricular lesson to be taught in the disciplinary process.

Morse v. Frederick (2007)

Morse v. Frederick (2007) dealt with a student who unfurled a banner reading "BONG HiTS 4 JESUS" at a 2002 Winter Olympics torch run. During this event leading up to the Olympics, a school principal allowed students to line the street in front of the school to witness the running of the Olympic torch past the school building. The event took place during the regular school day and was school-sanctioned. After seeing the banner openly displayed in public, the school principal confiscated the banner and eventually suspended the student (Frederick) for 10 days because his banner appeared to advocate illegal drug use—a clear violation of school policy. The student appealed his suspension to the school superintendent, who upheld it but limited it to eight days. The superintendent noted in his rationale that the student was suspended not because the principal disagreed with the banner but that the speech appeared to advocate the use of illegal drugs (p. 3). The student then alleged a First Amendment violation of his freedom of expression. The U.S. Supreme Court decided the principal did not violate the First Amendment when she confiscated the banner and suspended the student for violating the school policy. Through this limited holding, the court held that a school administrator may restrict student speech at a school event when the speech is "reasonably viewed as promoting illegal drug use" (p. 8).

While this case deals little with student violent writing, it does stand with the trio of other U.S. Supreme Court cases that deal with student expression. If nothing else, it presents an argument for school administrators to forbid student writing that promotes illegal drug use as a part of a classroom assignment. In addition, discussion in the case promotes the notion that school administrators should have latitude to discipline student expression simply because it occurs at an inappropriate time regardless of the message. That is, simply unfurling such a large banner at a school event was inappropriate alone, and an administrator should be able to act on that situation. While not binding case law, the discussion was had and opens some gray areas for increased administrator latitude on expression restrictions unrelated to the message being expressed.

How do these cases apply to classroom writing samples?

Consider the following student writing sample discussing current events:

> I think immigrants cause a lot of problems in our society. I mean, if you aren't here legally then why should you be allowed to stay? One big problem facing our society is providing public education to everybody. Schools are expensive to run and you should only be allowed to go to School if your parents pay taxes and you are in the country legally. Immigrants just cause problems, like lots of gangs and babies out of wedlock. I think illegal immigration is the biggest problem facing our country.

This piece of writing, on its face, discusses a controversial issue probably being discussed in government and civics classes across the nation. While under *Tinker* students are still allowed to have their own political beliefs, if this same sentiment was written in a class within a school that had had numerous student fights between immigrant groups, or within a community where there had been violent protests over illegal immigration or even if it caused the students in the class to become so disruptive that the class could not continue to be taught, the writing could be suppressed. Additionally, if the student had written the sentiments and created large posters with similar sentiments to post around the school building, such expression could be suppressed. However, if the tone of the class is to discuss current events, write your own thoughts about current events, and learn to have peaceful discussion about varying opinions, the writing could be allowed. The key with *Tinker* is not content of the message necessarily as much as how the content is interpreted and affected by the context of the message (the type of situation currently happening at the school, the "mood" of the school culture, or just the overall atmosphere of the school). The writing would also be allowed under *Fraser* because it is not lewd or vulgar and permitted as well under *Hazelwood* because it is part of the school's curriculum and obviously the opinion of one student. However, consider the next writing sample in the same current events-type class:

> I hate this fucking school and all the teachers. These halls are lined with illegals who don't deserve to be here. We'd be better off if you were all dead. Yo! Let's smoke some weed after school and see where it leads . . . I want to kill you all. Beware!!!

Tinker would allow this expression to be suppressed if there is a "likelihood of material or substantial disruption." Given the violent nature of the writing, the purpose of the assignment (to discuss current events) and the likelihood that students would become fearful, unable to learn, and disruptive to the school, the writing should not be allowed. *Fraser* would also permit this writing to be suppressed because it is vulgar, and because the school does have a "pedagogical concern" (such as teaching civil discourse, keeping peace among all types of students, promoting positive student culture), the writing could be suppressed under *Hazelwood.* It could also be suppressed under *Morse* because it is promoting illegal drug use within the school.

The True Threat Standard

In addition to the four landmark cases outlined previously, several circuit courts have applied something called the true threat test—or a way of testing to see if student expression is actually a threat to others or just a piece of graphic fiction. This is a difficult area for school administrators because there is no one method courts have used to define what constitutes a threat. A threat is generally considered some intention to commit violence against or harm others, but can be interpreted from two vantages—one from the speaker's stance and one from that of the recipient. Standing in each of these unique places can certainly change how a statement is interpreted. For instance, if one jokingly tells a coworker "If you eat that last cookie I'll kill you!" the statement could be misconstrued if the relationship is fraught with arguments about food or someone has recently been harmed for stealing sweets in the office. If the expression is determined to be what is called a true threat, or an intent to harm others, it is simply not protected by the Constitution. If it is not a true threat, then the expression, as graphic or gross as it presents, may be expression protected by the Constitution. Public schools, however, are difficult environments because all permissible speech in the outside world is not necessarily permissible within the walls of the school. Therefore, if the expression is not truly threatening, it is not automatically permissible and protected in public schools as the confines of the four U.S. Supreme Court cases are still applicable. Administrators are permitted to control expression that is materially disruptive, vulgar, lewd, or school-sponsored.

While it is clear that truly threatening speech is not constitutionally protected, lower circuit courts are divided in how to determine if expression is truly threatening. For instance, if a student writes "I want to kill him!" it might be useful to decide if the student actually intended the threat (if not, is it really wise to discipline a student for a joke or a random, stupid statement?) or if the recipient of the statement interpreted it as a threat (or was simply overreacting or misinterpreted what the adolescent student intended to say). Different judicial circuits decide if a statement is truly threatening in different ways. This means that the location of your school in a particular judicial circuit determines how you weigh the magnitude of apparently threatening student speech. Several circuit courts have applied the true threat test and have divided almost evenly as to how that test is applied.

The Court's Call for Citizenship Education

Public schools today are charged with more than just administering standardized tests or leading students through day-to-day activities. Courts and politicians have long noted that public schools play an important role in fostering and growing a democratic society. Schools do have duties under the law including compulsory attendance, adherence to state and national curriculum mandates, and goals set forth by localized school boards. It is sometimes easy to ignore that education is much more holistic in nature—it is more than solving math problems or studying historical facts. Education, through the venue of the public school, is a means of teaching students responsibility, morality, and the ideals of a democratic society. It can be argued that the goals of the public school are not necessarily outcome based through curriculum but are outcome based on the type of citizen the school produces.

When discussing teaching citizenship, morals, or values in public schools, the debate often ensues about whose values we are going to teach? Will we teach the values of the church down the street or the prominent political party in the country? How do we decide? Uerling (1999) argued that the question "Whose values do we teach" is misleading because the purpose of public schooling really encompasses two ideas: "First, we teach those values about which there is some consensus; second, we teach that there are some values about which there is little consensus and perhaps much controversy" (p. 207). In addition, schools are permitted to have expectations and regulations that foster a productive and nondisruptive learning environment. By setting forth an environment where students can explore controversial issues, can adapt or reject philosophical views, students learn to discover one of the major problems in the world—"that problems (in the world) are the result of people not treating one another well" (p. 208).

In 2011, President Barack Obama continued the revolving door of revised education planning in the United States. He reiterated the need for school reforms by stating, "A world-class education is the single most important factor in determining not just whether our kids can compete for the best jobs but whether America can out-compete countries around the world. America's business leaders understand that when it comes to education, we need to up our game. That's why we're working together to put an outstanding education within reach for every child" (Obama, 2011). The president proposed a reworking of the 2001 legislation commonly referred to as the "No Child Left Behind Act" enabling schools the flexibility to address notable achievement gaps. At no time has a president or congressional leader disavowed the important function of public school in shaping the country's future.

Citizenship Education Through the Curriculum

While politicians, judges, or philosophers do not solidly agree upon the exact design of citizenship education, it has still been taught, both formally and informally, in public schools for years. Yet no one curricular approach, program, or movement has been readily adopted or enforced as "the way" to help foster democratic growth in students. Schaps and Lewis (1998) proposed three qualities central to what schools could do to foster good citizens through citizenship education programs. First, schools should encourage a deep regard for self and others. They noted, "Good citizens are neither doormats nor narcissists, neither blindly self-sacrificing nor ruggedly self-serving. They speak up strongly for what they believe and want, but they also try hard to hear, to understand, and to accommodate the needs and perspectives of others." The second quality was the idea that good citizens are personally committed to justice and caring, so much so that their lives are models of action rather than inaction. Last, schools should teach students to interact in civil and considerate ways because interpersonal behavior reflects values. The authors noted, "Thus, the daily behavior of good citizens provides both lubricant and glue in our diverse, fast-paced society."

Several programs exist today to teach character formation and moral development. Following are some examples of available programs:

Character Education Program	Description
Rachel's Challenge	Started in memory of Rachel Scott, the first student killed in the Columbine shootings. This program and its training materials instruct students on how to be a positive person, treat people well, and instigate positive change in adolescent culture. (*Source:* http://www.rachelschallenge.org)
Character Counts	A popular nonprofit program in many public schools today touts itself as teaching kids a "framework for ethical living." The program consists of 6 "pillars" of universal values that schools incorporate into the daily lives of students. The "pillars," focus on trustworthiness, respect, responsibility, fairness, caring, and citizenship. Schools incorporate behavior strategies and incentive systems to encourage positive "pillar" behavior. (*Source:* http://charactercounts.org/sixpillars.html)
Boys Town Education Model	Boys Town provides a structured format of behavior expectations and response in its "Well-Managed School" series. The program boasts that it "promotes a model of teaching social skills across the academic curriculum, which enables students to assume responsibility for managing their own behavior." (*Source:* http://www.boystown.org/educators/workshops/well-managed-schools)
WiseSkills	An interdisciplinary K–12 program highlighting inspiring role models and nine character traits, including respect, responsibility, positive attitude, caring, self-discipline, trustworthiness, citizenship, conflict resolution, and fairness. Students work in advisory groups to study character themes present in the lives of real-life role models, including Aristotle, Florence Nightingale, and Maya Angelou. (*Source:* http://www.wiseskills.com/ Accessed July 1, 2012)

There are many more character education programs available to schools today and the ones identified here exemplify the common characteristics schools look for when purchasing a curricular model for behavior and moral development. These examples are cross-curricular and do not require schools to stop teaching core academic areas to allow focus on character development. Several programs integrate academic skills into the curriculum and behavior management system of the school. In addition, there is an overarching emphasis that character is a way of life, not just something that students do for a certain period of time and then stop. Character, moral development, and ethical decision making interweave in all aspects of a school and should therefore be a primary focus when discussing the true purposes of public schooling.

Courts Agree: Public Schools Are More Than Books and Pencils

The U.S. Supreme Court has not been silent on an overarching notion that schools are more than just buildings and routines. The court recognized that schools have a "mission" to complete and in order to do so those running schools must be given the trust and latitude to do so. As a brief illustration, consider the language set forth in the decisions from the four major U.S. Supreme Court cases dealing with student speech in public schools.

In *Tinker*, a landmark case from the 1960s, students silently protested the Vietnam War by wearing black armbands to campus. Administrators were fearful of the potential for disruption and forbade students to wear the armbands. In a successful First Amendment challenge by the students against the school, the court famously stated that "students do not shed their constitutional rights at the schoolhouse gate"(p. 506). The court looked back in history to a statement it made in an earlier school case: "The vigilant protection of constitutional freedoms is nowhere more vital than in the community of American schools. The classroom is peculiarly the 'marketplace of ideas.' The Nation's future depends upon leaders trained through wide exposure to that robust exchange of ideas . . ." (*Shelton v. Tucker*, 1960). The court saw the school and, more important, the interactions had at school, as an important tool in growing a diverse and vibrant population.

A 1986 case dealt with a lewd student speech presented at a school assembly. In *Bethel v. Fraser*, a school administrator disciplined a student based on the content of a racy and vulgar student council election speech. The student challenged the discipline under the First Amendment and the court sided with the school. Language in this case outside of the actual judgment itself is illustrative of the court's belief that public schools are more than storehouses for young children. It went on to state, "The process of educating our youth for citizenship in public schools is not confined to books, the curriculum, and the civics class; schools must teach by example the shared values of a civilized social order." The court relayed its intention that schools are some sort of vehicle for a future society adding, "The undoubted freedom to advocate unpopular and controversial views in schools must be balanced against society's countervailing interest in teaching students the boundaries of social appropriate behavior" (p. 681).

Hazelwood v. Kuhlmeier (1988) asked whether a public school is required to tolerate all student speech. The content of a school newspaper created in a journalism class was somewhat controversial and the principal decided to not allow the students to publish the paper (it dealt with such topics as divorce and teen pregnancy). The students unsuccessfully challenged the principal's actions and, instead, found the court agreeing with the administrative oversight of the school. The court argued that the speech in the school newspaper, produced as part of a journalism class, was "an integral part of the school's educational function." The court agreed the best judges of how to educate students are educators and parents, not judges. The case allowed schools to exercise discretionary judgment over school publications as long as the action was based on a "legitimate pedagogical concern" (p. 273).

The most recent U.S. Supreme Court case to discuss the role of public education was *Morse v. Frederick* (2007), a case involving disciplinary action against a student who unfurled a banner promoting drug use at a school event. In its support of the school's disciplinary action, the court stated, "School principals have a difficult job, and a vitally important one" (p. 2629). The justices noted that the principal's action, or inaction, would send a powerful message to the students at the event, signaling that administrators are charged with a great deal of responsibility for the overall culture of the school.

It is important to note that this body, the U.S. Supreme Court, is given the task to be the staunchest protector and interpreter of the U.S. Constitution. The justices are highly educated and well versed. Regardless of political affiliation or beliefs, it seems the court does agree that public schools are important for teaching students how to be constructive members of society. While the justices are not practicing educators, they have, through their decisions, acknowledged the tenuous position of being a public school educator and the importance of the proper, smooth functioning of a school in order to create and foster future citizens. The next chapter explores the importance of school culture and how you, as a school leader, can assess and change the climate and culture within your school building to preserve student safety.

Summary

Student expression can be controlled, especially if it is threatening. School administrators can rely on the guidelines set forth by the U.S. Supreme Court—principles that apply to all public schools in the nation. These guidelines are:

1. *Tinker* allows school administrators to suppress or discipline student expression that causes a "substantial disruption or material interference with school activities."

2. *Fraser* applies to student speech that is vulgar, lewd, or plainly offensive. Some courts require the student speech to not only be vulgar and lewd before applying *Fraser* but that it also occurs as part of a school-sponsored activity.

3. *Hazelwood* permits the school to suppress student speech that is inconsistent with its "basic educational mission," even though similar speech would be permitted outside the school. It also allows regulation of school-sponsored speech as long as the rationale is "reasonably related to a legitimate pedagogical concern."

4. *Morse* allows school administrators to suppress student expression at school-sponsored events that promotes illegal drug use.

In addition, truly threatening speech is not constitutionally protected. As discussed previously, however, administrators should contact their school attorneys to determine how their judicial circuit may test to weigh if something is viewed or perceived as truly threatening. In cases dealing with student violent writing, administrators should document the perceptions of those who read or received the writings in order to argue that the writing was perceived or understood as a threat to a student or staff member.

Judicial opinions, most notably those of the U.S. Supreme Court, penned by some of the nation's most intelligent thinkers, include language supporting the idea that public education is more than facts and statistics. The court, it seems, is telling us that public education is about teaching moral and ethical duties, as well as academic information. In fact, it acknowledges the difficult role of today's school administrator to make important decisions while leading a school.

Students learn more in school than math and reading skills. Schools are integral to creating an educated and involved citizenry. While today's schools struggle to meet national standards and assessment criteria, the goals of teaching values and morals should not be left behind. Schools are called upon by the nation's founders and judicial scholars to use the schools to inculcate the values necessary to be constructive and contributing members of the democracy.

Practical Applications for Teachers and Administrators

For K–6 Schools

- Begin teaching students about the Constitution and the Bill of Rights, and in particular freedom of expression. Emphasize to students how important these fundamental rights are and that with each comes a high degree of responsibility. Elementary school is the perfect time to tap in on student interest in learning about citizenship. As you celebrate President's Day, recite the Pledge of Allegiance, or study the Declaration of Independence. Provide opportunities to discuss how good citizenship affects the community.

- Model appropriate and acceptable expression at all times. Encourage parents and community members to do the same when you communicate with them. Emphasize good citizenship as a key component in your character education programs. Allow field trips where your students can practice good citizenship from visits to nursing homes to helping out at a local food bank.

- When a student swears or uses a "bad" word at school, have a brief discussion about the importance of words and how some words are inappropriate for school.

- Provide opportunities for students to practice being good citizens to the school—allow students to volunteer to help in different areas of the school and to complete tasks that we usually expect adults to do for us (emptying recycle bins, carrying important papers to the office).

- Create a student newspaper where students can learn skills about writing for an audience, editorial lessons, and publication responsibilities.

- Purchase high-appeal books for your school library about the First Amendment. These books should be current and colorful.

- Reward good citizenship. Promote good deeds by handing out "good citizenship" awards, medals, or having special recognition sessions. Make citizenship a source of pride in your building.

- Converse with your students about threatening language—and emphasize that threats are never jokes.
- Create school displays that teach about the First Amendment. Bulletin boards, media center book profiles, and posters of First Amendment principles should be visible throughout your school.

For 7–12 Schools

- Make sure you have a class offering at every grade level that focuses on First Amendment principles at some point during the year. Encourage teachers to incorporate citizenship education in every curricular area. Allow teachers to step away from state standards and proscribed curriculum and teach some citizenship skills.
- Provide hands-on lesson plans and teaching tips of ways teachers can incorporate teachable citizenship moments in class.
- Encourage students to participate in school newspaper classes or clubs. Be involved in this class and visit it frequently to discuss student writings.
- Purchase relevant and current texts (within the last two years) for your school library that discuss First Amendment issues.
- As you casually talk with students, ask them about current events and First Amendment newsworthy things happening in the news. Listen to their opinions.
- Create active and visual learning opportunities about the First Amendment—posters, essay contests, banners can all simply promote First Amendment principles.
- Never joke about threats with staff or students. Never use threats as jokes. Even if you know a student has expressed a threat as a joke (i.e., "Hey, Mr. Carter, I'm gonna kill somebody if there are sloppy joes in the cafeteria again this week!") Use this opportunity to explain this to the student in a meaningful, yet nondisciplinary fashion.
- Provide voting as a way to influence school change in nonadministrative ways (vote on a new lunch entrée, vote on a school celebration theme, etc.).
- Allow blood drives, food drives, and other community-focused events to take place in your school so students can actively participate.

- Revisit how you "crown" students—perhaps the students who should be "crowned" should earn that award for character traits rather than popularity.
- Be prepared to discuss First Amendment principles in disciplinary situations—especially those when students feel their First Amendment rights to free speech or free expression are being stifled. Take the key phrases from these cases, write them on a piece of paper and post them prominently in your office. Having the key language close by helps when you are called upon to defend why you are suppressing student expression.
- Provide opportunities for students to practice expression–whether it is writing contents, speech events, or drama skits.

Questions to Consider

1. What events would you consider to be "substantially or materially disruptive" in order to meet the *Tinker* standard to suppress student expression?

2. What language is clearly "lewd , vulgar, or patently offensive," and what language is foul, but not enough to meet this standard?

3. When you want to suppress a student's expressive conduct, either written or spoken, what will you say to the student? What will you say to parents or community members who challenge your decision?

4. Consider alternative ways to deal with student expression that could clearly be disciplined—and determine if more can be learned through alternative discipline strategies than suspension or expulsion.

5. How does your school teach character education and emphasize good character traits?

6. How can you incorporate discussions about good citizenship into your behavior conferences or school discipline plan?

7. Do your staff members model good character traits? How and when? What areas need improvement and why?

8. What is your personal philosophy of education and how does citizenship fit into that philosophy?

3

School Culture and Student Safety

Children can't learn if they are worried about their safety.
—Former First Lady Laura Bush

Identifying the characteristics of the "culture" of a school is a task that is often difficult to put precisely into words, but it is certainly something that intimately affects student safety. Imagine yourself as a middle school student again; do you remember the "popular" crowd? What about the "geeks" or "nerds"? Culture might refer to the atmosphere or attitudes within a school. It might denote the emotional connotations brought forth when mentioning an alma mater. Sometimes described as the climate or ethos of the school, the word *culture* is often used to describe the overall atmosphere of the school—how it makes you feel or the emotions evoked by walking in the doors. Deal and Peterson (1999) stated, "We believe the term *culture* provides a more accurate and intuitively appealing way to help school leaders better understand their school's own unwritten rules and traditions, norms, and expectations that seem to permeate everything: the way people act, how they dress, what they talk about or avoid talking about, whether seek out colleagues for help or don't, and how teachers feel about their work and their students" (p. 2–3). School culture affects everyone, from students to custodians, and school administrators need to be particularly aware of the signs and symptoms of a decaying or troublesome school culture. It seems logical to assume that students attending schools where the culture is demeaning, degrading, or tolerates discrimination struggle with productivity, positive contributions, or constructive behavior. Some studies in the late 1980s indicated that school culture is critical to the successful improvement of teaching and learning.

School culture influences more than just how students feel or respond after walking through the doors each morning. Deal and Peterson (1999) outlined six ways schools are affected by school culture, and among those was the idea that a positive school culture increases positive student behavior and schools that are optimistic, socially caring, and energetic have staff and students who take on those characteristics (p. 8). When considering how a negative school culture influences students, it is possible that a depressing or nonsupportive school environment actually increases the amount of negative student behavior, some of which is produced in student writing. It is important to understand the correlation between a negative school culture and the likelihood that one result will be violent or troublesome student writing. After all, if the students are miserable, it makes sense that their writing will reflect that misery, and if the students are comfortable and content, writing will reflect a similar notion.

What Students Write About (and What It Can Say About Your School Culture)

Students write about their lives and the events, people, and emotions that surround them. Therefore, school is a popular topic for those who spend a majority of their day in the school setting. Dylan Harris and Eric Klebold, the two teens that committed the Columbine shootings, were known to complain about their treatment by other students at school. In his personal journal, Klebold wrote about an angry man in black gunning down "preps." In fact, Harris and Klebold were known for their dark stories. Shortly after the Columbine incident, a public debate ensued about the social atmosphere at Columbine High School and rumors that Harris and Klebold were "goths" tormented by "jocks." An article published in *Salon* presented first-person accounts of adults who considered themselves outcasts like Harris and Klebold. One adult wrote about his high school experience, "I remember sitting in biology class trying to figure out how much plastic explosive it might take to reduce the schoolhouse—my biggest source of fear and anxiety—to rubble. I scowled at those who teased me, and I had fantasies of them begging me for mercy, maybe even with a gun in their mouths" (Cullen, 2009, p. 157). Certainly the volatility of adolescence can frame the school environment as a frightening place to encounter day after day.

Published case law involving violent or disturbing student writing is illustrative of exactly the types of issues students write about and how reflective the writing is about school culture. Consider the emotions behind the topics set forth in these documented student writing cases:

1. Suicidal tendencies (*Carrier v. Lake Pend School District #84*, 2006)

2. Disdain for feeling wrongly accused by a teacher (*D.G. v. Independent School District #11 of Tulsa County Oklahoma*, 2000)

3. Angst from being snubbed by a girl in class (*Jones v. Arkansas*, 2002)

4. Criticism of school administration (*Beussink v. Woodland R-IV School District*, 1998)

5. Feelings of anger toward a math teacher (*Boim v. Fulton County School District*, 2007)

6. A wish to blow up the school (*Cuff v. Valley Central School District*, 2008)

7. Anger and sadness over a pet's death (*Boman v. Bluestem Unified School District*, 2000)

Following is a list of common student emotions that led to student violent writings:

- Suicidal thoughts
- Feeling wrongly accused of something
- Feeling misunderstood by those closest to the student
- Being snubbed or bullied by classmates
- Boyfriend or girlfriend relationship problems
- Anger
- Dissent with school administrators or other authority figures
- Private violent thoughts
- Sadness

Undoubtedly, students write to express some pretty dark feelings. Therefore, it is vitally important that sometimes these writings may be a way of coping with the issue at hand yet also might be signs of trouble brewing in a student's mind. These writings can serve as a means of gathering information about a student when used in concert with personal interactions and staff reports of student behavior. By recognizing that students have real problems that cause real pain, an administrator can help open avenues of communication and relationships.

The U.S. Secret Service and the U.S. Department of Education studied school violence and created a guide to manage threat assessment in schools. This guide included some anecdotal writings from students about school culture illustrating just how culture of a school can impact a student:

> "What I hate about this school is that I'm being picked on in the halls and just about everywhere else." —A 14-year-old student.

> "School has always been hard for me, literally from the first day I started elementary school. People saw me as a . . . good target. They just started picking on me for no reason . . . they made fun of me [and, now] I'm going through self-esteem issues because of the 11 years I was a target." —An 18-year-old student.

> "They want me to open up, express myself. Quite a funny notion, ironic! If someone had helped me do that several years ago, I probably would have turned out okay." —Comment in a diary by a 17-year-old student who attacked others at school, then killed himself (O'Toole, 2000, p. 14).

Students will write about what they know best and it only makes sense that a student who spends 7 or 8 hours a day in school is bound to write about school experiences. Administrators must pay attention to what students write, not only for its content but also for the insights such writing can provide about the culture of the school itself.

The School Administrator's Influence on School Culture

One of the most important roles a school administrator has is in establishing and maintaining the culture of the school. Hoover and Oliver (1996) stated,

The research on school climate suggests that the principal is the most important person to have involved in school violence-reduction programs. Researchers have consistently reported that the principal's leadership and vision predict the degree to which the staff is able to effect needed reform, particularly in discipline matters (p. 38).

Whitaker (2003) also noted that "effective principals viewed themselves as responsible for all aspects of their school" from budgeting to teacher morale (p. 16). In addition, effective principals hold themselves responsible for the overall climate in their building. Skiba (2000) reported one way administrators could establish and maintain a positive school climate is to have a set of procedures in place to deal with student threats. Included among several suggestions were the importance of a well-established working relationship with local law enforcement, a set of preplanned responses within the school building, and the importance of dialogue throughout the school community that all threats will be taken seriously. By having these discussions beforehand, an administrator creates a climate wherein students are aware of the severity of making a threat and the competence of the school to handle a threat when one is made.

School culture and climate, though, is not the sole responsibility of the principal. In 2011, the National School Boards Association put together a toolkit to help school boards have climate and culture conversations with students. This set of questions helps school board members casually and purposefully interview key cross section groups of students, asking questions such as "Do you feel safe at school?" "Have you been bullied at school?" or "Do you feel respected by staff and students at this school?" During this conversation, students are encouraged to share honest observations about the climate and conditions of the school's daily life.

School culture is more than living out a school motto or mission statement. The culture of the school can be uncovered in virtually any area: the expectations of the school (both implicit and explicit), the rituals of the school, school traditions, teacher histories, building architecture, dress codes, and how students are treated by the school staff and other students. It permeates people, walls, and traditions. It shows people how to act, how to feel, and how to respond. It is evolutionary and an extremely strong and invisible force within a school. Kupchik (2010) wrote about his perceptions of his own school experience in his book *Homeroom Security*:

Yet as overwhelmed as I felt (as a teenager), I imagine that I would feel even more stress if attending the same public high school today, since schools in the United States have changed so dramatically since then . . . Today's public schools are rife with strict rules and punishment, including zero-tolerance policies, random searches by drug-sniffing dogs, high suspension rates, surveillance cameras, and the presence of police officers. I didn't get into trouble while in high school, so even with today's discipline regime in place I probably wouldn't have been suspended or arrested. But had I passed by an armed officer every day, been subjected to searches by a team of dogs, or walked underneath the constant gaze of security cameras, my awkwardness and discomfort within my own skin would probably have been even greater (p. ix).

School culture undoubtedly influences student learning, staff behaviors, and the overall "feel" of the school; however, it is important to note the impressive role school culture plays in fostering a safe school environment. After all, if a student is worried about getting into a fight, being punched in the locker room, being harassed by another student, or being shot by a stranger, it could be quite difficult to focus on math and science. Student safety is a primary duty of the school, for without it, learning cannot take place. That being said, schools are generally one of the safest places to be during the day for most U.S. students.

Salazar (2008) detailed the "high-impact school leader" and noted that these leaders create a school that "fosters belonging." This included teacher communications with students, administrative interactions with students, and an overall belief that students throughout the entire school are safe and cared for. In addition, these leaders also help students learn to cope with adversity and crisis, providing workshops and after school programs to help students develop social skills and support strategies (p. 43).

The Secret Service and U.S. Department of Education threat management guide included guidance for creating a "safe" school culture. This included fostering a culture of respect, creating meaningful connections between adults and students, breaking the "code of silence" kept by many students unwilling to bring outsiders into potentially violent situations. The guide provided a set of components that administrators should consider for creating a safe school climate, including assessment of the school's emotional climate, prevention of bullying, development of trusting relationships, and developing a mechanism for creating a safe school climate (Fein et al., 2002, p. 13).

Improving Your School Culture

School culture is not stagnant, and as an administrator you are not stuck with the school you inherited from the previous administrator. In fact, the culture of a school can change multiple times within a day. Consider this description of the school administrator from Deal and Peterson in the Jossey-Bass Educational Leadership Reader (2001):

> Everyone watches leaders in a school. Everything they do gets people's attention. Educational philosophy, teaching reputation, demeanor, communication style, and other characteristics are important signals that will be read by members of the culture in a variety of ways. Who school leaders are—what they do, attend to, or seem to appreciate—is constantly watched by students, teachers, parents, and members of the community. Their interests and actions send powerful messages. They signal the values they hold. Above all else, leaders are cultural "teachers" in the best sense of the word (p. 201).

Read about school culture and utilize online resources to investigate what students and staff feel about the environment in your school. One of the things noted in the Columbine High School investigation was that the school principal, Mr. D. was well-liked and could peruse the hallways seeing the happy faces of students—all leading him to believe undercurrents of bullying and mistreated students were being handled appropriately. While he was doing his job, he was simply unable to get an accurate read on the culture of the school (Cullen, 2009). As an administrator, you cannot read the minds of the students and staff in your building, but you can stop to ask questions about how these groups feel they are treated, how the school is serving their needs, and how things could be improved. And it is not too late to start asking these questions; even if you reside in a toxic school culture, you can start asking questions, visiting with students, and redefining the expectations within your building.

Skiba (2000) reported the importance of the school administrator's role in establishing a positive school climate. One of the most important roles an administrator has in maintaining a positive school climate is to have a set of procedures in place to deal with student threats. Included in several suggestions were the importance of a well-established working relationship with local law enforcement, a set of preplanned responses within the school building (for example, an intervention by a school counselor), and the importance of dialogue throughout the school community that all threats will be taken seriously. By having responses prepared even before a threat occurs, an administrator creates a climate wherein students are aware of the severity of making a threat and the competence of the school to handle a threat when one is made.

One school superintendent relayed a list of qualities a principal should have in order to gain student trust and build a positive school culture. He stated,

> A principal should be almost constantly visible. He or she should be visiting a classroom every single day and should be visible during all hall passing times. He or she should focus on forming relationships with students that are not friend-ships, but are significant and trusting ones. He/she is engaged with the school faculty to make sure they know relationships are important. Last, the principal should have firm and fair discipline policies so that students know what to expect (M. Lineburg, personal communication, January 10, 2012).

It was apparent from my conversation with this former principal and current superintendent that sitting in an office and waiting for a problem to arise was one of the worst behaviors a school administrator could do.

Summary

When students walk into a school, the first thing they experience is the culture and climate of the school building. The overall feel, tone, and atmosphere can dictate whether a student thrives or falters within the school environment. Teachers and administrators are integral in fostering a positive school culture and do so by proactively providing opportunities for students to be heard, for changes to be made, and for the climate to be constantly reevaluated. Students tend to write about what they know—and school culture is something that they are keenly emotionally affected by. Therefore, we must carefully assess student statements about school culture so that we are in tune with the student perception of the school's culture and where we might be able to influence positive change. In addition, the next chapter explores the larger concept of school policies and why a zero-tolerance policy is not the best approach to dealing with student violent writing incidents.

Practical Applications for Teachers and Administrators

For K–6 Schools

- Create and administer a school culture survey at least once per semester. Study the results and determine areas of improvement.
- Be visible in your school and use these opportunities to study the culture and climate in your school.
- Be vigilantly on watch for teachers or students who are destroying school culture. Do whatever you can to intervene immediately.
- Begin discussing bullying issues. Topics might include how to respond to a bully, how to respect each other's differences, and how friends treat each other.
- Teach Internet safety and responsibility to students and parents. Consider using an Internet filter on school computer equipment or teaching responsible Internet safety on open campuses.
- Create social groups or some other type of forum where students can talk about culture and climate issues to trusted school personnel on a regular basis.
- Be explicitly clear about appropriate and inappropriate school conduct especially to younger children who may be unable to read social cues or understand the complexity of group dynamics.
- Provide opportunities for older students to form positive relationships with younger students, like buddy-reading times or multiage or level character education groups. Remove age barriers when discussing school culture issues so that it is seen as a building issue and not just a classroom issue.
- Administrators, be present in classrooms daily. Teachers, be active in your classroom. Do not use class time to check e-mail or do tasks that can be completed after school. Use class time to build relationships with students.
- Use visual displays to express excitement and positive sentiments about learning and school.
- Communicate positive sentiments with parents through your school communications. Tweet inspirational messages; include positive quotations in your school newsletter. Let the messages that leave your school express passionate excitement about students and learning.

For 7–12 Schools

- Be visible during passing times and before and after school. Use these times to converse with students, listen to their stories, and have fun. Smile.
- Think about implementing a dress code.
- Attend school activities even when you are not required to—this shows your commitment beyond your usual job duties.
- Create and administer a school culture survey. Interpret and act on the results.
- Allow your student council or similar student government group to be actively involved in school policy guidance.
- Create social groups where students from different grade levels meet weekly or monthly to discuss character education topics or do problem-solving exercises.
- Provide opportunities for older students to mentor younger students through tutoring sessions or classroom volunteering activities.
- Be vigilantly on watch for teachers or students who are destroying school culture. Do whatever you can to intervene immediately.
- Provide a safe reporting avenue for students to report bullying or threats.
- Teach Internet safety and responsibility, including lessons on cyberbullying and the ramifications for posting personal or derogatory things online. Consider using an Internet filter on school computer equipment or teaching responsible Internet safety on open campuses.
- Have students create and run a school pride campaign.
- Invite alumni to participate in school activities and to bridge the gap between student and graduate. Demonstrate the school as a community rather than a limited year engagement in one's life.
- Dedicate resources to track students who are performing poorly in school or have a lackluster attendance pattern. Once identified, personally intervene with each student and set up a plan that involves staff contact as issues are worked through.

Questions to Consider

1. What things do you do to promote a positive school culture? Where do you need to improve?

2. What do you think students, parents, and teachers think and say about the overall culture and climate in your school?

3. How do your students and teachers know you have high expectations?

4. How can you show students and teachers that you are fair and firm in your administrative actions?

4

Regulating Student Expression

Examining Your School Policy

Censorship feeds the dirty mind more than the four-letter word itself.
—Dick Cavett

Regulating student expression is often confused with suppressing student expression. While school administrators are frequently looking for reasons to discipline a student based on the content of his or her expression, such actions are often mistaken for censorship or suppression, and this is often cast in a very negative public light. The First Amendment clearly provides students some expressive freedom while at school, but this freedom is not a wide entitlement to say or write whatever happens to come to mind. As an administrator, one has to be confident and careful when assessing and disciplining student expression within the school.

Why a Zero Tolerance Approach Fails Everyone

School administrators are often seeking methods for fair, efficient discipline. It is common for schools to have policies regarding student threats that institute suspensions or expulsions. However, some schools, especially in the immediate years following the Columbine events, began instituting zero tolerance policies for violent or graphic student writing. Zero tolerance policies hold the potential to over-reach into protected student speech. A zero tolerance policy exercised when a student creates a piece of violent writing is a black and white approach to a rather gray problem. Zero tolerance means no investigation, no conversations, no teachable moments; it simply asks if the student did the writing and institutes an automatic punishment for the content of the writing.

A zero tolerance policy is a policy that mandates a set consequence or punishment for a specific offense regardless of the rationale for the offense. Zero tolerance policies generally came into public awareness with the adoption of the federal Gun-Free Schools Act of 1994. Under this legislation, a student who possessed a firearm or bomb on public school grounds was required to receive a one-year expulsion. Eventually deemed unconstitutional, the effects of this law exist in legislation seeking to end bullying, harassment, and threats. Zero tolerance policies, when applied in the strictest sense, often appear ludicrous. Skiba (2000) wrote about a Florida student suspended for ten days when she loaned her nail file to a friend at school. In Louisiana, a student was expelled for one year for possessing one Advil tablet in violation of her district's zero tolerance policy (Schoonover, 2007, p. 233). The get-tough approach behind zero tolerance policies is meant to deter students from engaging in threatening behavior yet does not allow for individual circumstances that might underlie a student's actions. Atkinson (2005) stated that advocates of zero tolerance policies want to "send a clear message" and protect students. She noted a 2004 Public Agenda survey of teachers and parents found support for zero tolerance when dealing with "persistent troublemakers" and for enforcement of "little rules" that help set the tone and atmosphere of a school (p. 3).

Zero tolerance seems easy to implement but actually is quite troublesome when dealing with student violent writing. First, if a student has written something violent or threatening for a classroom assignment, there are several things that need to be investigated: Why did the student write the piece? What were the instructions given by the teacher assigning the writing? Were there implicit or explicit instructions that may have contributed to a student writing such a piece? What was the teacher's initial response? In what context was the piece created? What was the teacher's curricular rationale for the assignment? What was the student's motivation or rationale for the writing? Quite simply, there are a lot of questions that need to be asked and answered.

The Consortium to Prevent School Violence offers some suggestions about zero tolerance policies. First, an administrator should understand that unfair or unjustifiable harsh penalties, such as a zero tolerance policy, might result in a poor school culture or cause an administrator to act in a way that is contrary to the best interest of the student involved. Second, administrators should avoid using the term *zero tolerance* so as not to create the impression that they are inflexible or unable to consider the circumstances regarding the totality of the student's conduct (Peterson & Schoonover, 2008, section 5).

It is important to note that governing bodies of several national educational associations do not endorse zero tolerance policies. The National Association of Secondary School Principals supports zero tolerance policies but only if the policies allow discretion when implementing discipline. The group advocates considering the age and gender of the offender, ensuring the discipline is appropriate for the infraction, and continuing educational services throughout an expulsion or suspension. The American Bar Association adopted a similar stance asking that schools implementing zero tolerance policies also exercise discretion on a case-by-case basis.

Zero tolerance policies also have some pretty nasty side effects. This can include harsh penalties for minor incidents, disproportionate application of discipline to minority groups and special needs students, and questionable constitutionality. However, zero tolerance policies are comforting to some administrators. Peter Baluvelt, president of the National Alliance for Safe Schools (NASS) stated, "There are a lot of administrators who are comfortable having no discretion, especially when they have to discipline the mayor's child. It's much easier to say they must treat all kids the same because of zero tolerance laws" (Koch, as cited in Atkinson, 2005, p. 9).

Incorporating Legal Principles Into School Policies

Administrators can definitely discipline students based on the content of their writing, particularly if it takes place on or enters the school campus. Administrators and teachers do not have to allow students to write whatever they want, whenever they want and they should also not be fearful of exercising the ability to restrict student speech. The four U.S. Supreme Court cases outline the types of expression a school administrator can restrict. *Tinker* held that school administrators can restrict expression if it causes a "substantial disruption or material interference with school activities" (*Tinker v. Des Moines Independent School District*, 1969). *Fraser* permits school administrators to restrict student expression that it deems "vulgar and offensive terms in public discourse" and that occur when students are members in a captive audience (*Bethel School District No. 403 v. Fraser*, 1986). *Hazelwood School District v. Kuhlmeier* (1988) allows administrators to restrict student speech when it is school sponsored so long as the rationale for restricting the speech is "reasonably related to legitimate pedagogical concerns." *Morse v. Frederick* 2007) allows school administrators to suppress student speech that appears to promote illegal drug use. School policies governing student expression should also incorporate a statement that truly threatening speech is not protected speech and will not be tolerated within the school environment.

Sample Policies

School policies governing student expression tend to use the same legal keywords found in the U.S. Supreme Court student expression cases. Some sample policies from around the nation include the following:

School District	*School policy governing student expression*
Jefferson County Public Schools (Colorado)	Students have the right to assemble and express themselves by speaking, writing, distributing, wearing or displaying symbols of ethnic, cultural, or political values such as buttons, badges, emblems, and armbands; or through any mode of dress or grooming style; or through any other medium or form of expression, except that the principal, or designee, may regulate expression, provided the regulation is based on legitimate educational concerns, there is a factual basis for believing a specific form of expression by a specific student is causing or will cause substantial disruption of school activities, or the expression constitutes a health or safety hazard. Students shall also have the right to refrain from expressing themselves in these student-originated activities. (*Source:* www.jeffcopublicschools.org/publications/conduct_code.pdf)

New York City Department of Education	The department's discipline code includes statements that students are to "refrain from obscene and defamatory communication in speech, writing, and other modes of expression in their interactions with the school community," and to "express themselves in a manner which promotes cooperation and does not interfere with the educational process." (*Source:* Citywide Standards of Intervention and Discipline Measures, NYC Department of Education, p. 11, Sept. 2011 from: http://schools.nyc.gov/RulesPolicies/ DisciplineCode/default.htm)
Lincoln Public Schools (Nebraska)	This district provides a brief policy statement regarding student expression that reads: "The Lincoln Board of Education recognizes the legitimate rights of students to exercise their expression of ideas under the Constitution of the United States. At the same time, the District reserves the authority to make reasonable rules pertaining to students' exercise of free expression, access to school facilities, and use of school equipment." (*Source:* Lincoln Public Schools Policy and Regulations, retrieved from http://www.lps.org/about/policies/ Policy 5501)
Kansas City Public Schools (Missouri)	This district's Student Code of Conduct identifies levels of student behaviors and classifies those behaviors into offense categories. Class I offenses are those which disrupt the learning environment but are normally not severe enough to need a referral to administration (these are generally handled by the teacher). A class I offense can include obscene behavior or the use of profanity, which is defined as "the use of any language or actions, written, oral, physical, or electronic, remark or expression, including obscene gestures, which is offensive to modesty or decency, in violation of community or school standards" (p. 14). More severe Class II and Class III offenses include more vague categories like "Disrespect" and "Inappropriate Computer/Internet Use" which includes "accessing, communicating, or creating inappropriate and/or profane information" (p. 16). (*Source:* Kansas City Public Schools Student Code of Conduct, http://kckps.org/code/)

School policies should outline proscribed behaviors necessary for a functioning learning environment. Ineffective policies are ones that are lengthy, too specific, or overly vague. At a minimum, your school policy should include language supporting regulation of student expression that is materially or substantially disruptive, that is lewd, vulgar, or obscene, that is school sponsored, that promotes illegal drug use, or that is threatening. Steer clear of vague terms such as *offensive* or *appalling*. Stick to the guidelines that a court will support if challenged and be clear that each situation will be handled on a case-by-case basis with individual investigations conducted for each incident.

Summary

Disciplinary approaches to student violent writing incidents should be grounded in sound school policy and should avoid a zero tolerance approach. While school policies should be sure to provide due process and protect student constitutional rights, policies should also seek to provide students the ability to rehabilitate or revise student writing in order to learn from the incident. While policies are overarching and apply to the student body as a whole, the unique nature of the writing classroom itself and how student violent writings might be created within your building are explored in the next chapter.

Practical Applications for Teachers and Administrators

For K–6 Schools

- Create a working list of alternative disciplinary actions that do not include suspension or expulsion, such as conferencing or cooldowns. Circulate this list to your staff and practice implementing when appropriate.
- Create and adhere to high expectations for students, both academically and behaviorally.
- Identify and study your school district's student expression policy. Break it down into smaller chunks and begin to educate students on appropriate behavior in minilessons or sprinkled throughout your curriculum.
- Explain the concept of zero tolerance to students and explain to them that there are certain behaviors that will not be permitted no matter what.
- Reward positive behaviors through tangible prizes or certificates.
- Allow students to make mistakes. When they do, explain the behavior, why it was wrong, and how it could have been modified to be appropriate.

- Do not attach a student's poor behavior to the student as a person. Separate the two and allow the student to be a kid.
- Implement productive and responsive communication strategies for teachers and parents; publicize e-mail addresses, require biweekly communications from teachers, and always respond to phone calls and e-mails within 24 hours.
- When a student has a behavior problem, forget quickly. While you may document and keep track of behavior incidents, do not remind the students of past poor behaviors or treat the student as if you expect them to misbehave daily. Instead, show the student that each day is a fresh start and a new opportunity to have a great day.
- In your case-by-case dealings with students, show a positive and caring spirit. Use encouragement whenever possible. Be flexible and fair at all times.

For 7–12 Schools

- Find your district's student expression policy and use it as a teaching tool for students.
- Create and adhere to high expectations for students, both academically and behaviorally.
- Brainstorm a list of disciplinary actions that do not include suspension or expulsion. Print these actions on a list that can be easily accessible when you need to consider how to discipline a student. Be flexible and fair at all times.
- Model a caring approach in disciplinary situations. Listen and keep calm at all times.
- Allow students to make mistakes and use disciplinary scenarios as moments to teach appropriate behavior and expectations.
- When a behavior problem happens, forget quickly. That is, while you may have documented a student's behavior problems, do not give the impression to the student that you expect bad behavior in the future. Give the student a chance to have a fresh start daily. Pretend as if the previous day never happened.
- Implement productive and responsive communication plans for parents and teachers. Require teachers to communicate biweekly, have school phones answered by real people (not machines), and require all e-mails to receive responses within 24–48 hours.
- Track students with long disciplinary histories and assign a counselor or trusted staff member to meet with the student weekly. Begin a proactive approach to student discipline. When

a student discipline situation arises, ask the assigned staff member to participate if possible.

- Steer teachers away from having zero tolerance classroom policies. Instead, help teachers write clear expectations that have specific consequences.
- Create opportunities to personalize learning. Find ways to implement independent study options, school-within-a-school possibilities, and updated and modern curriculum options.
- Reward positive behavior—such as awarding local fast-food gift certificates for catching someone doing a good deed.

Questions to Consider

1. Can you find and understand your school district's student expression policy? If not, who can you contact to help?

2. Do you use a zero tolerance response to any behaviors in your school? If so, are you getting your anticipated results?

3. How do you communicate your expectations to staff, students, and parents?

4. Where are your strengths and weaknesses when dealing with student behavior issues?

5

Violent Writing Within the Classroom

Words are the most powerful drug used by mankind.

—Rudyard Kipling

Student violent writing can emerge anywhere at anytime. The writing might be penned during a student's free time—on a Web page, a blog, a journal, or a note to a friend—or it might be drafted in response to a classroom assignment ("Write about a time you had a conflict with a friend . . ."). Consider some of the topics (war, racism, sexual development, social issues) and texts ("Romeo and Juliet," *Lord of the Flies, I Know Why the Caged Bird Sings*) taught in today's classrooms. Additionally, life outside of school is not a perfect world. Some of today's students pass through crime-ridden neighborhoods on their way to school or return home to violent family conditions at night. Troubled students might have witnessed murders, assaults, or rapes. Today's adolescent has more electronic access to violent video content and graphic texts than ever before—some at the touch of a button on their cell phones. If we ask or want students to write authentically, about things they know best, then it is simply unreasonable to expect students today to write in a way that is only pleasing to the adults reading the content. Student violent writing may emerge in fiction or nonfiction, off campus or on campus, in first person or third person. The generation of the writing itself cannot be controlled. Therefore the response must be cohesive and well planned.

But what makes a student write violent, gory, dark, or disturbing content in the first place? Is it always a deranged student on the verge of committing a horrendous crime or can it be a creative venture of a true artist? How are schools teaching writing that would lead a student to even have the opportunity to write violent content? What are teachers doing to control violent writing? Writing itself is an art. Words formed into a sentence and eventually into a story can move a reader to a new environment, can evoke untapped feelings, and can create visions of unimagined places. Writing itself is an art unlike any other skill taught in school and should be treated as such.

Freewriting Is Not the *Cause* of School Violence

Many English classrooms today utilize the practice of freewriting, or writing without stopping to concern oneself with the content or grammatical structure of the words on the paper. A teacher might instruct students to write about the biggest problem facing teens today and a response might look like this:

> Drugs are the biggest problem facing teens today. I mean, its not that hard to get drugs anywhere, anytime. I think it is real hard for teens to deal with peer presure . . . its hard being a teenager .. i mean with your parents breathing down your neck and grades and all ..... heck . . . maybe just being a teenager is the biggest problem . . .

Or it might look like this:

> This damn school is the biggest problem facing teens today. The stupid dumbshitprincipal who walks around like he owns the place and the dam detention becuz i was late to p.e. three times. if I didn't have to show up at this stupid place I would be soooooo happy..i can't wait to get out of here and tell everyone in this school to kiss my ass

The responses can vary from student to student, day to day, hour to hour, and mood to mood. And this lies not with the practice of freewriting—which some students might find somewhat cathartic—and not necessarily with the student response, which many students will use to express appropriate emotions for a school setting. The problem lies with the few students who express violent thoughts and may or may not consider carrying those thoughts into action. Consider the writing of Allen Lee, a Cary, Illinois senior whose English teacher directed the class to write without worrying about self-censorship. Lee's response, in the form of an essay called "Blood, Sex, and Booze" stated,

> My current English teacher is a control freak intent on setting a gap between herself and her students like a 63 year old white male fortune 500 company CEO, and an illegal immigrant . . . And baking brownies and rice crispies does not make up for it, way to try and justify yourself as a good teacher while under-handedly looking for complements on your cooking. No quarrel on you qualifications as a writer, but as a teacher, don't be surprised on inspiring the first [Cary-Grove] shooting (In his own words, 2007, para. 5).

Is freewriting a sound teaching practice? Absolutely. The concept of freewriting or writing without self-censorship is introduced in the first chapters of most student writing textbooks. The task is presented as a way for student writers to explore ideas without censoring the thought process. Basically, write whatever's on your mind and you can come back and change it later. Do not worry about spelling or grammar—just get the idea on paper. Such exploration fosters creativity and ingenuity. If students are allowed to write about whatever they want in whatever way they want, they might discover a new character, a new plot line, or simply a new way of describing the same old thing. Most writers use this stage as a means of getting ideas on paper and then revisiting the ideas later to weed out the good ideas from the bad. Macrorie (1985) discussed the personal investment a student makes in writing and admitted that many American children are often a "victim" of strict, traditional teaching methods in the English classroom. He noted that students are taught to write one way in school, a traditional formulaic way, while outside school they are engaged in writing that is more relevant to the world, such as letters to the editor.

Textbooks aimed at English teacher education promote the idea of freewriting as a proper means of teaching the writing process. Three times in their textbook, *The English Language Arts Handbook: Classroom*

Strategies for Teachers, Tchudi and Tchudi (1999) suggested the concept of freewriting as a class activity. The authors encouraged teachers to use freewriting and instructed teachers to:

> Establish a freewriting or journal-writing day, preferably once a week, on which students can write about anything in life.... Read students' work with an aim to better understand who they are and what they care about; then look at the writing itself for evidence of language skills. This self-selected writing should not be corrected.

No matter what kind of writing course it might be, no matter what the age group, students will benefit from the freewriting exercises, the model of the writing process, the advice of self-management based on that model, and the techniques for finding out what words do to actual readers (p. vi). A key to teaching freewriting is also to teach students the concepts of *purpose* and *audience.* That is, why are you writing what you are writing and how would an audience perceive or respond to your writing? Freewriting, in and of itself, should not exist without also pairing it with these important concepts.

Writing as a Predictor of Violence

Violent writing *can* be a sign of a violent student, but it is not necessarily a predictor of violence. It is important, however, that educators be aware of the warning signs of teen violence, including the types of writing that are sometimes practiced by violent students. Phil Chalmers (2011), author of *Inside the Mind of a Teen Killer,* compiled a list of general indicators of a troubled teen. These included the following:

- Making a statement or direct threat about harming or killing others
- Being fascinated with weapons
- Coming from a violent family
- Keeping a journal, a Web page, or other art forms filled with violent writing
- Being bullied and mistreated by others, especially at school
- Suffering from anger problems or depression
- Preferring isolation (p. 176)

The FBI and Secret Service have similar lists of possible traits of troubled youth. The lists, while descriptive and illustrative, are also a problem because school officials cannot use them as reliable check-lists. It is simply impossible to know for sure which student who writes about violent content will act on it and which student will not. Therefore, while the urge is to forbid violent content altogether, it is more realistic to accept the notion that some violent writing is a predictor of violence, while some is not.

Writing Instead of Violence

Writing, as a practice, can also be utilized as a form of therapy or violence prevention. Writing, after all, is completely self-driven and created by the author. Without the author, there is no story. Shortly after the Columbine incident in 1999, Nelson (2000) wrote a plea to schools to allow English teachers to help prevent violence through writing. Nelson noted, " . . . teaching writing is teaching the use of language . . . Language is both the source of much violence in our society—and its potential cure." Nelson's theory called for a return to the personal story in the writing classroom. That is, writing in many schools has become formulaic and predictable—the five-paragraph essay, the author biography. Instead, the author calls for a more personal, peace-driven writing classroom. Consider the depth of the author's statement:

> In a society where our own voices cannot be heard over the shouting of commercials and the blare of entertainment and within a curriculum that values a heartless critical essay over personal story, our stories sit in us, waiting to be told, to be acknowledged. Untold and unacknowledged, they will eventually translate themselves into other languages—languages of abuse and addiction, of suicide and violence. In such a society and in such schools we are literally dying to tell our stories. The tragedy at Columbine High School, like all such violence, was a publishing of untold stories, unheard needs, and unhealed hearts (pp. 43–44).

Writing is also used as a self-growth and self-understanding tool. It is not uncommon for a mental health counselor to ask young patients to write how they feel about something on paper or to express their anger or despair through written words. In Alabama, professional writers and corrections officials have partnered in "Writing Our Stories," an antiviolence writing program where students publish their therapeutic writings in an anthology. Young girls often cherish the privacy of their locked diaries, not because of the extrinsic value of the book itself but because a diary is a place where one can express personal thoughts, dreams, and disappointments. Writing is more than a process and more than a word count; it is a highly personal investment and one that, if properly tended to, can help students contribute to a school rather than withdraw from society.

The Unique Nature of the Writing Classroom

Just as the climate and culture of the school impacts each student's experience within the building, so too can the atmosphere of each classroom—particularly English and Language Arts classrooms and those where similar writing activities take place. The English classroom is frequently the place in the school where discussions about life, morals, ethics, ideals, and principles are explored through writing and literature. Burke (2003) called the English classroom a "crucial forum for discussions about values, ethics, and morality" (p. 390). It is in the English classroom where texts are dissected, ideas are debated, and values challenged. The American Library Association's list of "100 Most Frequently Challenged Books" did not include a math or science text for good reason. The 100 books are story based, and it is the content of these stories that causes conflict to the conservative challengers. It is only logical for the English classroom, where novels and stories are central to the core fundamentals of the class, to be the place where values are discussed and ethics explored. After all, how can you read *Huckleberry Finn* without discussing race? How can you read *Of Mice and Men* without discussing loyalty or friendship? The tasks in an English classroom call for exploration of the most intimate parts of the human soul.

In addition to reading, discussing, and exploring moral and ethical topics as a class, students also have the opportunity to use writing to explore their own thoughts about topics brought up within the class. Burke (2003) wrote:

> Writing is the heart of the English class. In one form or another it is constant: We are reading it, doing it, or preparing to do it. Writing invests students with an authority that challenges them to ask themselves, and express in language, what they know. Few things give me greater satisfaction than watching a student's voice and style grow and improve over the course of a year. This close attention to students' writing is what makes writing so important in my class: It is through our conversations about their writing, their ideas, even their

lives that I come to know my students. These talks, which might take place in my class or in the margins of their papers, form a private space where my students and I meet to discuss their development as writers—and as individuals. It is here, in the drafts, notes, and clusters, that we watch our students compose their lives and try on different voices, as they cast off one draft or another of themselves, in search of the voice they will recognize as their own (p. 141).

Students use writing not only as a function of learning content but as a means of expressing disappointment, betrayal, secret desires, and aspirations. It is in the English classroom where students write about their families, their summer vacations, and their best friends. Blystone (2007) wrote:

> Students, like just about anyone else, usually express them-selves in the form with which they feel most comfortable. If a student is an artist who likes drawing cartoons, he or she may use that medium to express rage. If a student is a writer, he or she may draft a fictional children's story to indicate angst (p. 209).

Students sometimes write about extremely personal topics. Unlike math or science where a formula may find a specific numeral answer or lead to a successful experiment, writing at times has no right or wrong, no limit to the imagination, and sometimes no censor-ship. The writing teacher must be an artist—one who can carefully compose a mural of discussion, mind expansion, and self-reflection while fostering students to become mature, conscious decision mak-ers within the confines of the rules of the school and the expectations of society.

"But, Teacher, I want to be the next Stephen King."

I've always appreciated the debate that ensues when the concept of limiting or censoring student writing within a school emerges with a discussion about popular horror author Stephen King. Students and teachers trying to defend violent or graphic writing will sometimes say something like, "You shouldn't stifle student writing . . . after all, what if that kid is the next Stephen King? Wouldn't that be a shame?"

King has authored over fifty novels, many filled with fright and horror. But King, himself a teacher, acknowledges the sensitive environments of schools today. He once discussed violent and graphic writing in response to a 2007 shooting on the campus of Virginia Tech. King acknowledged that in today's world, violent writing has to be considered much more seriously than when he was in college in the 1970s. In an Entertainment Weekly commentary, he acknowledged that his own writings in college would certainly have raised red flags about him in this "sensitized day and age." He recalled one of his own students who had written extremely violent stories that caused King himself to be concerned. The student, a quiet and unassuming bookstore clerk, was one whose writing caused King to note to himself, "Whoa, if some kid is ever gonna blow, it'll be this one." King, in fact, is somewhat critical of students who write graphically with no heart, stating that it is almost impossible to pick out which graphic authors will become the next killer unless you look for writing "unenlivened by any real talent."

The Lost Lesson: Purpose and Audience

It is tempting to isolate freewriting into its own class of writing and to admonish it as a poor teaching strategy. Freewriting, though frequently witnessed as one of the earliest lessons in writing textbooks, is often paired with the *subsequent* lesson in the writing book titled "Considering Purpose, Audience, and Tone." When students freewrite as part of the writing process, they are generating ideas. However, writing texts also instruct writers to consider the audience they are writing for, the purpose of the writing, and the tone needed to achieve their writing goal. That is, if a student is brainstorming ideas for new after school clubs, it would behoove the student to think about who will eventually receive the list of ideas (the classroom teacher, perhaps it will be read aloud to the class, perhaps it will be sent in letter form for the principal to consider when revamping clubs available at the school). In addition, the students should think about the tone of the writing needed to communicate effectively with the intended audience. Purpose and audience are two extremely important lessons that should be taught with all writing in all content areas; the concepts form a trilogy of good writing strategies for all writers: brainstorming, purpose, and audience. If a writer thoughtfully considers all three of these concepts and accurately assesses the needs required in each of those steps, a very detailed conversation can occur between a teacher and student or administrator and student when discussing why a student wrote a violent essay or topic.

Advice for All Teachers of Writing

So if the problem with student violent writing is not within the teaching methods, what then is a writing teacher (or any content area teacher who utilizes writing as an instructional component) to do? Teachers should continue to use writing activities such as brainstorming, journal writing, and freewriting. Former English teacher and current public school superintendent Dan Endorf described the conundrum faced in schools today. He stated,

> As long as there have been schools, there have been teachers dictating directions prior to beginning assignments. Today's society demands that teachers add another element to this process by clearly stating the difference between the author writing for creativity and the author being sequestered in the principal's office for inappropriate, threatening language. Plainly said, too many horrible events have taken place in schools for this generation of teachers not to make these statements prior to the writing process. It's also important to create assignments that don't tempt students to write with offensive language. Careful consideration must be given during the development of the assignment that directs students away from themes of violence (D. Endorf, personal communication, January 10, 2012).

Some innocent writing assignments have resulted in student violent writing, and we have to acknowledge the potential is there. A few guidelines can be helpful when designing writing practices in any classroom:

- Consider setting limits on what may be written in journals, including announcing what may be off-limits and subject to administrative referral. While drafting a list of off-limits topics will never cover every conceivable topic, it can help set the tone of expectations within the classroom. A statement such as "violent themes in your writing must be appropriate to be shared with others. If it is not, it may be subject to further administrative review." Basically, do not design writing assignments as a complete free-for-all with absolutely no expectations or ramifications for content.

- Be cautious about having "private" sections of student writing. The National Council of Teachers of English suggested teachers allow students to have a "Do not read" portion within their writing journals in class. This practice can be troublesome if the writing within foretells violent events that are actually carried out. While teachers should not be expected to read every single word a student writes, allowing students to create private and protected areas within the classroom may undermine school safety.

- Be prepared to create a written policy about violent writing and to share that policy with administrators, parents, and students. The policy might be as simple as "All writing must be appropriate for class. Inappropriate writing will result in a student/teacher conference and may result in administrative referral." It is best to be vague and general so as not to limit your ability to respond to student violent writing.

Summary

Writing practices such as journal writing, freewriting, or stream-of-consciousness writing are valid, sound teaching methods when used appropriately. Teachers should continue to use these methods with some attention to setting boundaries within the classroom. Administrators should be aware of the unique nature of the English/writing classroom. Within the walls of this classroom, students discuss morality, ethics, and other highly personal topics. It only makes sense that their writing reflects the content of the class. All teachers, not just writing teachers, should be prepared to discuss their expectations and classroom policies with their school administrator before the school year begins. It is possible that the student you censor or discipline for violent writing may just be the next Stephen King, but even Stephen King has noted that teachers should pay careful attention to the content of student violent writing in today's schools.

All writing teachers should have thorough yet nonspecific policies regarding student writing that include statements informing students that troublesome writing may lead to teacher or administrator intervention. However, not all student violent writing occurs within school. Sometimes that violent writing targets the school administrator. The next chapter deals with issues of writing beyond the classroom, including when the writing targets the school administrator.

Practical Applications for Teachers and Administrators

For K–6 Schools

- Promote creative writing. Allow students of all ages, from emerging writers to proficient writers, to have a journal or creative writing notebook.
- Teach brainstorming, purpose, and audience as a trilogy. That is, when students are freewriting, teach them to also think about whom they are writing for and why they are writing. Frequently discuss this concept.
- Model good writing practices. Yes, that means you. Stop checking your e-mail and write with your students. Show students that you enjoy writing and also think about whom you are writing for and why you writing.
- Foster a reading culture. Reading improves writing and through reading you can discuss the writing trilogy with ease; include the purpose of a writer's piece and identify the intended audience of the writing.
- Form an administrative and counseling team to be on call when student violent writing emerges. Be prepared to assess whether a student is a threat.
- Allow counselors to use writing as a therapeutic tool.

For 7–12 Schools

- Promote creative writing as a regular course offering. Some schools have creative writing classes or creative writing units within specified classes. Encourage creativity as a positive trait.
- Frequently engage in discussions about the parameters for writing in schools with students; discuss why some topics might cause problems in today's schools. Help students understand your side in the issue and listen to their thoughts.
- Encourage reading in all content areas and through reading discuss the concepts of purpose and audience.
- Identify an administrative and counseling team that will respond to student violent writing. This team should be prepared to begin a threat assessment procedure immediately.

- Allow students to write as an alternative to talking (even in behavior conferences). Some students will feel more comfortable discussing difficult issues through writing and you may learn more when you allow a student to write their feelings or perceptions of an event.
- Model good writing. Go into classes occasionally and complete the same writing activity the students are doing. Use these opportunities to build relationships.
- Prepare students to understand the limits of writing within a school. That is, teach brainstorming in conjunction with lessons on audience and purpose.

Questions to Consider

1. Do your students use freewriting or journaling in your school? If so, what expectations are conveyed to the students?

2. What are your personal writing habits and preferences? How do those influence how you govern a school?

3. Examine the atmosphere of your English and Language Arts classrooms compared to other classrooms in the school. How are these classes different than other classes in your building?

4. What individual classroom policies do your teachers have about violent writing? Are these appropriate now that you've read this book?

6

Violent Writing Beyond the Classroom

When I was young I thought that people at the top really understood
what the hell was happening . . . now I know they don't know.

—David Mahoney

Administrators today are troubled by more than student violent writing that is penned during the school day. With the emergence of social media, blogs, Internet access on cell phones, and communications sites like Twitter, students may actually be writing more today than ever before. With this writing come more dilemmas for school administrators. This chapter addresses the three most prominent issues in today's schools: off-campus writings, cyberbullying, and writings that target the school administrator. Even though these writings seem to take a different form than words on paper, the response of the school remains virtually identical.

Off-Campus Writings

Dealing with student violent writing would be much simpler if it all occurred within a classroom and in response to a classroom assignment. Unfortunately, very little of the student violent writing that occurs in schools fits that profile and an administrator must be keenly aware of the difference between violent writing that occurs on school grounds and that which occurs online or off school grounds. Student expression that occurs off school grounds is granted greater protections than that which occurs within the confines of the school. Generally, writing that occurs within a school can interfere with the proper functioning and order of the school day. Off-campus expression does not necessarily interfere with the school and therefore is protected with greater scrutiny.

These lines—of where writing originates, is discovered, or causes a disruption—are often blurry, and there are no firmly established rules for administrators to follow. In addition, courts across the country are divided as to whether schools are able to discipline students for off-campus student writings. Consider these most recent cases:

Cases Where Schools Prevailed

- *D. J. M. v. Hannibal Public School District* (2011), where a Missouri student was suspended for sending an instant message from his home computer to another student's home computer detailing his desires to get a gun and kill some students at their school. The Eighth Circuit Court of Appeals held that this student's speech was a true threat and not protected by the First Amendment, but even if the First Amendment had protected it, the school had the authority to discipline expression with effects that "reverberated to the classroom."

- *Kowalski v. Berkeley County Schools* (2011) involved a student who created an extremely derogatory MySpace page on her home computer about a classmate. When school administrators were alerted to the situation, they suspended the student for several days. The student argued that the school had no right to discipline her based on writing she created at home. The federal court disagreed and noted that while the Supreme Court has not dealt specifically with discipline parameters for off-campus student writings, it did find support in *Tinker* (1969) that a school has the authority to discipline conduct that interferes or disrupts the work of the school.

- *Doe v. Pulaski County Special School District* (2002) found a heartbroken Arkansas student writing a series of letters over summer break about a girl who had dumped him. The letters were violent and expressed his desire to rape and murder the girl. The student's best friend acquired one of the letters from him and read it to the targeted girl during gym class that fall. The girl was frightened and informed school officials of the content of the letter. The student was expelled and challenged the expulsion. On review, a federal district court determined the contents of the letters to be true threats and unprotected by the First Amendment. This allowed the school to discipline the student for the content of the letters even though the letters were written at home with no intent to ever deliver the letters.

- *Doninger v. Niehoff* (2008). A Connecticut student lost a First Amendment battle when she was disciplined for calling her school administrators "douche bags" in an online blog post. Unhappy with some administrative decisions, Doninger took her opinions online. Part of her online blog directed readers to call the school to complain about the administrative decisions. Administrators disciplined Doninger by not allowing her to run for student office. A federal appeals court agreed that the administrative action was appropriate in light of the comments and that Doninger's blog post was "potentially disruptive to student government functions."

Cases Where Students Prevailed

- *Layshock v. Hermitage School District* (2007). This student created an offensive MySpace parody page of his school principal basically pretending to be the principal and commenting negatively about the principal's large physical frame. The student faced disciplinary action and sued the school for violating his First Amendment rights. Eventually, a U.S. Federal Court of Appeals found the student's postings did not meet the "material and substantial disruption" standard set forth in *Tinker* nor did schools have the right to punish off-campus speech even if it rose to the "lewd, vulgar, or indecent" level set forth in *Bethel v. Fraser* (1986). One comment in the case stated, "It would be an unseemly and dangerous precedent to allow the state, in the guise of school authorities, to reach into a child's home and control his or her actions there to the same extent that it can control that child when he or she participates in school sponsored activities."

- *J. S. v. Blue Mountain.* Another principal parody page was the subject of this case, where an eighth grader was suspended for her MySpace profile of her school principal describing his "Interests" as "fucking in the office" and "being a tight ass" among other colorful activities. The principal, obviously offended by the content of the page, disciplined the student, and the same U.S. Federal Court of Appeals that dealt with *Layshock* held that the threat of substantial disruption did not occur under the *Tinker* standard and therefore was protected expression.

These are only examples of the myriad of cases dealing with student off-campus speech, and the issue is simply not settled. As recent as 2012, the U.S. Supreme Court refused to hear arguments on a trio of off-campus student speech cases, leaving school administrators wondering what to do. As an administrator, this illustrates the need to document any disruption caused by the off-campus writings, to deal with off-campus student writings in a problem-solving mode as opposed to a disciplinary fashion, and to always report off-campus threats to law enforcement, because true threats are never protected speech.

Cyberbullying, Texting, and Facebook Writings

Cyberbullying, texting, and social networking all provide new and varied venues for students to practice their expressive writing skills. However, the principles remain for the school administrator. If the writing is threatening, it can be disciplined. If it materially or substantially disrupts the educational process, it can be disciplined. If it is authored during school hours, consider disciplining the student for violating your school's electronic use policy rather than for the content of the speech (to eliminate any possible First Amendment challenge). If the written conversations occur off campus but spill into the school and cause fights or cause a teacher to be unable to teach, you may be able to discipline the writings.

Cyberbullying, usually traced to Internet writings, can be disciplined if threatening. In addition, it is sometimes a symptom of a larger school culture and climate problem, sometimes one that school officials are completely unaware exists. Slonje and Smith (2008) noted three challenges schools face when dealing with cyberbullying: the inability of the victim to escape cyberbullying at school or at home, the wide audience targeted by electronic devices making it impossible to determine the extent or reach of the communications, and the anonymity of the cyberbully. While these challenges seem insurmountable, Couvillon and Ilieva (2011) found that cyberbullying programs taught at the school level were the most effective programs to date and the authors describe these programs as "a proactive schoolwide approach" rather than an after-the-fact reaction. Several useful suggestions for a schoolwide cyberbullying prevention program include having a specified staff person for cyberbullying reporting, providing staff training on cyberbullying issues, enforcing a clearly communicated commitment to digital safety, and defining and enforcing consequences for cyberbullying (p. 99). As an administrator, stick with the same principles for responding to any student violent writing: Document the writing, converse about the writing, listen to those involved, and respond to the writing swiftly and appropriately. You should strongly consider offering school-based professional development on identifying and dealing with bullying issues, including cyberbullying issues. The main legal issue schools face is doing nothing about cyberbullying. When it is brought to your attention or you have knowledge it is occurring, you must do something. Doing nothing is negligent and can expose your school district to risk should student harm or suicide occur. It is impossible to stop all bullying, so you should strongly consider implementing a bullying prevention program and providing safe places for students to report bullying to a trusted and delegated staff member.

When the Violent Writing Targets You

There is a visceral urge to respond with disciplinary actions when the student violent writing involves you, the teacher or administrator of the author. I have conversed with administrators across the country who have been called names such as "prick," "fucker," "asshole," "bitch," and "whore" online. This is not uncommon and has become a more prominent issue lately due to the emergence of online communication tools. These scenarios, pulled from actual case law, provide illustrative documentation of the emerging issue:

- A student creates a parody social networking page with your yearbook photo and writes an introduction that includes these statements:

  HELLO CHILDREN yes. it's your oh so wonderful, hairy, expressionless, sex addict, fagass, put on this world with a small dick PRINCIPAL I have come to myspace so i can pervert the minds of other principal's to be just like me. . . (*J. S. v. Blue Mountain*, 2010)

- A student copies your photo from the school website and creates a social networking page wherein he pretends to be you, writing you can't remember your birthday because you are "too drunk to remember" and responds to the question "In the past month have you ever been skinny dipping?" with the statement, "big lake, not big dick" (*Layshock v. Hermitage School District*, 2007).
- A student creates a Facebook page pretending to be you and claims to have sexual contact with students ("School principal cyberbullied. . .").
- A student draws a picture during free time in class depicting a gun held to your head (Anonymous teacher).

When you are being portrayed falsely or criticized (rightly or wrongly) online, it is important to stay calm and respond rationally. Imagine being the Arizona teacher whose junior high aged students wrote a list of methods they could use to kill her. This list included, "Tie a brick around her neck and drop her in a pool; run over her with a large truck, tie her up with ropes, suffocating her to death and set her on fire, and tie her up and put a dead butterfly in her mouth and have a recorder playing her voice over and over again until her head explodes and then set her on fire" ("The letter police said Chandler . . . ," 2011). Students have been criticizing their teachers and administrators for decades; it just has not been as prominent or noticeable as it is in the online forum. It stings and it hurts. It is okay to acknowledge that publicly posted criticism is often not fair. However, you must respond in a clear-headed fashion. First, contact law enforcement if you are being threatened or if you are being impersonated. Law enforcement can investigate any criminal charges or stolen identity procedures. Second, contact your school attorney immediately and provide any and all evidence of the online writings. Your school attorney may discuss possible civil claims that could be brought against the student on your behalf if necessary to protect your reputation. Next, determine and document if the page is actually causing a substantial or material disruption to the functioning of your school. If it is, you may have the ability to discipline the student. Last, if appropriate, conference with the student author and investigate the motivations and circumstances of the criticisms. However, it may be wise to not respond at all—which is only a decision you can make in conjunction with your school attorney. Regardless, students who post negative images, criticisms, and portrayals of school administrators or teachers often do so because they feel comfortable behind the alleged anonymity of the Internet. By conversing face-to-face with a student in a reasonable manner, perhaps that anonymity is lost and the student will realize the implications of his or her actions. In addition, several students in the cases noted here created the pages because they felt disconnected with the school or mistreated by the administrator, so it is important to address those issues immediately.

Staying Informed

It is imperative for all school administrators to stay up-to-date about student violent writing issues and student expression issues altogether. Here are some organizations and publications that regularly address these issues and provide legal updates specifically tailored to public school administrators:

- **Education Law Association.** A national nonprofit education law organization appropriate for all levels of educators. ELA publishes the *School Law Reporter* monthly in addition to a quarterly publication, *ELA Notes*, both of which highlight recent case law. ELA also offers numerous publications for member purchase. You can learn more about ELA here: http://educationlaw.org
- **Council of School Attorneys.** A branch of the National School Boards Association, this group provides legal advocacy and education for educators and legal professionals. COSA offers school law boot camps, webinars, a Twitter feed of breaking legal news, and a weekly newsletter of recent school law case summaries. You can learn more about COSA here: http://www.nsba.org/cosa

In addition, be sure to join your state-level administrator organization and local school law attorney groups. If nothing else, discuss these issues with your school attorney regularly.

Summary

Students will always have new and surprising ways to use and abuse writing. As administrators, with writing or any other issue in a school, your own learning is not stagnant and you must be continuously watching trends and adapting to new phenomenon. Recent innovations like social networking and text messaging have created new forums for student writing, and some of it has been hurtful to other students and to administrators on a personal level. It is always important to remember the legal principles that apply and protect schools: Speech that "materially or substantially interferes" (*Tinker*, 1969) with the function of the school, lewd or vulgar speech, and school-sponsored speech are the easiest to regulate. Off-campus expression is much more difficult to regulate, and it is even more complicated because it remains legally unsettled. In addition, there are the personal attacks on us as educators that cause us to want to ignore the Constitution altogether and defend ourselves at all costs. It is imperative to stay abreast of current education trends and education law developments by maintaining a strong working relationship with your school attorney and with professional development organizations directed solely at educating principals on legal issues in schools. Communicating with teachers about student violent writing should be a priority as you enter a new school year. The next chapter provides guidance on how to have these conversations.

Practical Applications for Teachers and Administrators

For K–6 Schools

- Consult with your school attorney to determine the legally permissible standard for dealing with off-campus student writings.
- Even if you are in a legal jurisdiction that is reluctant to let schools discipline student writing, you do not have to ignore it when it occurs. You may not be able to suspend a student for it, but you can conference with a student about it, inform parents about it, and use it to teach a lesson as to the scope of one's online presence.
- Teach a directed cyberbullying program. Utilize curriculum that teaches the definition of cyberbullying, how to report cyberbullying, and how it affects other people.
- Identify a trusted staff member for students to report cyberbullying or online attacks to.
- Protect your own online presence. Model appropriate online communication techniques. Do not communicate with students through personal e-mails and do not post inappropriate pictures of yourself online.
- Teach Internet etiquette, including how to use the Internet constructively.
- Find a trusted colleague to vent to when someone attacks you online. Remember, you are often criticized privately, so be prepared to see it in writing online.
- Prepare a way to calmly and civilly meet and converse with your online critics if possible and appropriate. Open yourself to listening to their complaints and finding a way to redirect them to address you personally rather than online.

For 7–12 Schools

- Consult with your school attorney to determine the legally permissible standard for dealing with off-campus student writings.

- Be prepared to discuss off-campus writings with students. Even though you may not be able to discipline some off-campus writing, you can still converse with students about the inappropriate nature of the writing or the reach of their Internet conduct.
- Teach Internet etiquette in every grade level. This can include Internet safety, cyberbullying awareness, and understanding the expansive reach of online postings.
- Model appropriate online behavior. You should not converse with students through personal e-mails or communications. In addition, your "image" online should always be professional. Do not post personal pictures of your bachelor party or night in Vegas.
- Be prepared for online criticism and identify a trusted colleague who can talk you through the hurtful comments.
- Prepare a way to calmly and civilly meet and converse with your online critics if possible and appropriate. Open yourself to listening to their complaints and finding a way to redirect them to address you personally rather than online.
- Identify a trusted staff member or protocol for students to report cyberbullying.
- Provide educational sessions for parents to learn more about Internet safety and new technologies.

Questions to Consider

1. How are you emotionally prepared to respond to harsh online criticism?

2. What is your school doing to combat cyberbullying?

3. Is your school adequately and explicitly teaching about online safety and Internet etiquette?

4. What professional organizations would best serve your need to learn more about legal trends and issues in education?

7

Communicating With Teachers About Violence in Student Writing

Any genuine teaching will result, if successful, in someone's knowing how to bring about a better condition of things than existed earlier.

—John Dewey

To effectively handle student violent writing situations, administrators and teachers need to have a common understanding of what is expected from each other, what types of writing should be reported, how violent student writings are reported, and the protocol for dealing with the writing. This is not simply the teacher passing the writing along to the principal's mailbox; a common dialogue must take place in order for schools to protect student rights and student safety.

Conversing With Teachers Before the School Year Begins

Education expert Todd Whitaker (2003) noted two ways a principal can improve a school include getting better teachers and improving the teachers you have (p.8). It is important for principals to know the habits, personalities, and writing instruction practices of teachers in every department. In today's digital culture where students are inundated with violent gaming, graphic song lyrics, and gruesome movie images, administrators need to initiate a conversation with teachers and staff members about appropriate student writing. My experience conversing with school principals about this topic seems to be quite forceful: "Well, the principal should be telling the teachers that students can't write about X, Y, and Z." Simple enough but really not dealing with the problem, and quite honestly, how could one ever draft an exact list of forbidden topics? A better approach is to focus on improving student writing through sound practices while having a plan to handle student violent writing in place.

Topics principals should discuss with teachers before the school year begins include the following:

- When he or she expects a teacher to turn over a piece of student writing (see more in Chapter 8 regarding the types of student violent writing)
- Documentation required from the teacher to explain the context of the writing (What was the assignment? What did the student say? What other things do you know about this student that might help illustrate the context of the writing?)
- The overall expectation of writing within the school—not avoiding writing because of the potential for student violent writing but of preparedness to deal with the situation if it arises
- A clear plan that the administrator will follow when he or she takes over the student violent writing incident

English and Language Arts teachers will probably take particular notice of administrators' increased attention to the content of student writing. And while writing instruction is often credited to and passed off to the English department, student violent writing can emerge in any classroom at any time. English methods professor Jim Burke (2003) instructs teachers in today's schools to be prepared for the administrator/teacher conference by compiling materials with an outline of rationale for why the teacher has chosen to teach a lesson in a particular way. Take the time to have a discussion with your English teachers (and your entire staff as a whole) about your thoughts about student violent writing. Describe your concerns with student writings you've faced in the past. Share your desire to protect student safety. Having this one-on-one conversation with teachers or departments will help build rapport while illuminating teacher practices for the administrator.

Recognizing Potential Syllabus Problems

Even if you are not a writing instructor, you can easily spot problematic syllabus statements in your teacher policies. Ask teachers to remove these three types of classroom policies that can be problematic for student writing:

1. One that promises "confidentiality" or "personal-use only" that somehow leads students to believe that no one will read what they have written in school. Classroom assignments should not be like diaries, and it is in the best interest of the school to not create an illusion of protection around student writing.

2. One that tells students outright to "write about whatever you want, without censoring your thoughts and without worrying about consequences." While this may be a great brainstorming activity, it should be done as just that, not used as a regular classroom policy. Even the National Council of Teachers of English (NCTE) suggests teachers set limits on what may be written in journals, including announcing what may be off-limits.

3. One that is overly strict and threatening. For example, "You should never write about anything I don't approve first," or "Please do not expect to use creativity in our classroom." While problem prevention may be the motivation, threats tend to chill student writing (and writing improvement for that matter).

Reviewing Teacher Classroom Policies

Administrators should require every teacher to turn in a set of classroom policies and should *read* each of those policies before the beginning of the school year to weed out inappropriate, overreaching, or ineffective classroom policies. As a classroom teacher, there were several semesters when I simply changed the date on the top of last year's classroom policies and turned it over to my administrator. One year, after carefully reading through the policies, I realized I had an outdated discipline procedure, an erroneous grading scale, and rules that I simply did not need. Administrators should consider requesting and possibly requiring teachers to formally address the issue of student violent writing by including a simple statement such as, "Writing is encouraged and practiced in this classroom. If your writing is violent, graphic, obscene, or disruptive to the class, I will contact your school administrator for further assistance." English teacher Jim Burke (2003) described the policy he uses with his writing students that read:

> *A Note About Confidentiality:* I encourage you to take risks in your journal writing: Write in ways you have not before. Be willing to be honest in your thinking or emotions when you write. I am not saying you should tell me all your deepest, darkest secrets. Nor am I telling you to refrain from writing about personal subjects (if you feel the need to do that). But you must realize that the law requires me (and I would want to anyway) to report anyone who tells me that someone is hurting them, they are hurting themselves, or they are harming others (p. 177).

Teacher policies should be kept on file so that if a student does write a violent piece and claims the teacher gave no specific limits for the assignment, the administrator can consult the specific teacher's policy handout to see if this would, in fact, be part of the teacher's express practices.

Suggesting Teaching Methods When You Are Not a Writing Teacher

So you see a teacher is being way too liberal with creative license and may even be encouraging student violent writing—what do you do? First, take the time to read your state's writing goals, standards, or expectations. Read the student writing textbook used in your district. Gain an understanding for the outcomes for the content of the classroom you are visiting. By doing this you are able to understand the curricular goals of the classroom, regardless of the content. Next, visit the classroom—frequently. Get a feel for what is really going on in the class. Is the teacher really telling students to write about a gory event involving the school cafeteria, or is the teacher instructing students on how to create vivid imagery in an appropriate context? Observe how students interact in the class; are they getting along or is the culture tense and bothersome? Then, meet with the teacher immediately to discuss what you observed. Express your concerns, discuss your expectations, and document your discussion. It is better to do this in an advisory capacity rather than a disciplinary capacity. Whitaker (2003) stated that the principal is a key factor in ensuring teachers accept responsibility for what goes on in the classroom. By maintaining open communication, asking questions, and visiting classes, an administrator can avoid being blindsided by student violent writing in response to a classroom assignment.

Continuing the Conversation

Student violent writing is not a topic reserved only for beginning of the year conversations. Brown (2011) studied the prevalence of student violent writings in some North Carolina high schools and one interesting trend that emerged from her study was that English teachers generally feel unprepared to deal with student violent writing when it occurs. Continue to dialogue with your staff about school climate issues, threat assessment protocol, and concerns they face about student behavior. Student violent writing can arise in any classroom and in any context (student assignment, random notes on a paper, in texts sent during class, or on social network sites outside of school). Recognize that student violent writing emerges at unexpected times, from unexpected students, and often in unexpected ways. Assure your staff you are prepared with a plan to handle any student violent writing and that you expect them to be vigilant in assessing, assigning, and promoting responsible student writing.

Summary

Student violent writing does not only happen in the English classroom. Any student can produce it at any time in any classroom (or anywhere for that matter). Administrators and all teachers need to discuss this issue before the school year starts. Collect and read teacher policies. Visit classrooms. Educate yourself on unfamiliar teaching methods and intervene in overly permissive writing environments. The next chapter provides specific guidance on threat assessment for student violent writing incidents.

Practical Applications for Teachers and Administrators

For K–6 Schools

- Converse with teachers about their writing practices and philosophies. Meet individually with teachers before the school year begins. Identify where consequences for inappropriate writing fall within their classroom behavior policies.
- Review adopted textbooks and study how the texts teach brainstorming and creative writing techniques.
- Allow students to share writings. Do not allow teachers to tell students their writings will not be shared or are private.
- Participate in writing instruction professional development sessions that teach writing across the curriculum.
- Do not allow teachers to promise confidentiality to students.
- Use time at team meetings or Professional Learning Community (PLC) meetings to discuss writing policies and practices at each grade level.
- Visit classrooms frequently to observe the conditions of writing and types of writing your students engage in daily.
- Subscribe to professional publications for elementary writing teachers; stay aware of new trends and alert to possible problems.

For 7–12 Schools

- Collect and document classroom policy documents. Meet individually with teachers before the school year begins to review these documents for policies that may help or hinder the writing process.
- Be on the lookout for free-for-all writing experiences. Discuss the purpose and ramifications of such activities with the teacher leading the activity.
- Do not allow students to have private writings as part of school activities.
- Do not allow teachers to promise confidentiality to students.
- Visit classrooms frequently to observe your teachers' writing lessons and activities.
- Meet with your English department to discuss creative writing teaching within the department. Determine if their practices are conducive to student safety and free expression.
- Subscribe to professional publications for writing teachers; stay aware of current teaching trends and writing practices.

Questions to Consider

1. What are your personal writing practices and beliefs? How do you think writers learn? What do you enjoy or dislike about writing?

2. Do your teachers allow freewriting without limits? How can you find out?

3. How would you converse with students who want to write violent themes in school?

4. How familiar are you with your teachers' classroom syllabi and policies dealing with writing? Do you actually read these and insist on changes when you see the need? Should you revise your policy review process?

5. What expectations do you convey to your teachers about writing within your school?

8

Threat Assessment for Student Violent Writing Incidents

Although the risk of an actual shooting incident at any one school is very low, threats of violence are potentially a problem at any school. Once a threat is made, having a fair, rational, and standardized method of evaluating and responding to threats is critically important.

—O'Toole, FBI, 2000

Just as schools today participate in a variety of threat assessment activities for armed intruders, bombs, or natural disasters, so too should schools have a protocol for investigating and communicating about student violent writing incidents. *Threat assessment* is having a plan for the unexpected events that arise in a school, and student violent writing rises to the level where a communications protocol and well-versed action plan is necessary. O'Toole (2000) stated, "The process of threat assessment rests on two principles: (1) all threats and threateners are not equal, and (2) most threateners are unlikely to carry about their threats" (p. 1). The threat assessment model set forth by the Federal Bureau of Investigation that dealt with all potential threats within a school included the notion that there is not a one-size-fits-all threat assessment plan, but the practice drills contained in many threat assessment plans allow schools to consider the "what ifs" and prepare a response for any situation that arises. Administrators and teachers should hypothesize, practice, and carry out a mock student violent writing episode so that baseline problems are eliminated before actually having to use the plan for a live event.

The concept of *threat assessment* was described as "strategies to determine the creditability and seriousness of a threat and the likelihood that it will be carried out" (Jimerson, Brock, Greif, & Cowan, 2004, p.1). Because there is no one single factor that predicts school violence, administrators should study what we know about school violence and use that information to prepare themselves for any potential violence that may erupt in their schools. One example of this might be the concept that, while all school shooters behave differently, most generally tell someone about their plans. By studying what is already known about school violence, administrators can begin to formulate a plan to respond to situations of hearsay, private conversations, or journals where a student has indicated a desire to bring weapons to school or to cause harm to oneself or others.

Redfield (2003) noted that student writing is often a sign that a student is prone to commit a violent act at school. She proposed a threat assessment procedure that schools could use when determining whether to discipline a student for the content of so-called threatening speech. The protocol included questions to be answered by the school administrator dealing with a threat made at school and included things like whether the student had a history of personal trauma, whether the student intended the message to be threatening, or whether the student had a trusting relationship with an adult. Redfield based her protocol on FBI and Department of Education research that showed students who commit acts of violence at school often communicate the intent to do so. One aspect she focused on in terms of student speech and threats was that a school administrator needs to determine the difference between a threat made and a threat posed. A student may make a threat but have no intention or ability to carry it out. However, determining if a student poses a threat requires a focus on student behavior, including a student's home life, personal situation, social networks, history of violence, and mental health status (to name a few). Redfield's main focus was that research tended to show that students who committed acts of violence at schools often communicated those intents in writing. She noted from the CDC, "over half of the incidents of violence that they studied followed a danger-signal such as a threat, note, or journal entry" (p. 668). Redfield stated, "We need to develop an ability, somehow, to distinguish between speech that constitutes a serious threat, and speech that is merely a cause for concern" (p. 668).

The United States Secret Service and the U.S. Department of Education published a report in May 2002 specifically dealing with threat assessment. "Threat assessment in schools: A guide to managing threatening situations and to creating safe school climates," included an action plan for school leaders to help foster safe schools and to logically assess threats. Included in the threat assessment tool was a way to identify students of concern, including a scenario where "A student submits a story for an English assignment about a character that shoots other students in his school" (Fein et al., 2002, p. 45). The assessment tool recommended an investigation into the life of the student, including discipline background, living situations, and relationships with adults (p. 49). In several of the threat assessment steps, the administrator looks for signs where the student writer communicated an expressed desire to harm himself or herself or warned others of the potential for an attack. The report implied writing could be a key factor in determining if a student is a threat, because many violent students will write about their targets or their desire to harm others prior to actually carrying out a plan. Because threatening situations are often chaotic and require acting swiftly, having a written plan for assessing student violent writing may eliminate confusion on the administrator's part and may help show students, parents, and teachers that there is a plan in place to ensure a safe school environment.

Appendix A in this text provides a well-written threat assessment protocol designed by doctoral student Lori Brown (2011). This protocol provides a series of step-by-step instructions for English teachers, administrators, and school personnel to follow in order to allow a student to receive due process while providing a thorough investigation into a student's motivation, background, and potential problems in order to conclusively draw safe assumptions about the reality of a student threat. Virginia professors Cornell and Sheras (2006) also created a school-specific threat assessment procedure as a result of campus shootings at Virginia Tech University. The tool is meant to assess any student threat of violence but contains another useful illustration of how any threat can be handled within a school.

Assessment Does Not Mean Profiling

There is a temptation to assume that "assessing a threat" really means "profiling" students based on their appearance, peer group, or odd adolescent tendencies. Educators notice trends in students and are well aware of the "in" crowd or the "loner" groups. Yet most educators have also personally known students who fit a traditional profile yet were nothing like the profile their appearances portrayed. I once taught a student who dressed very "Goth" and as such, I made some broad assumptions about her peer group. Ana wore heavy black makeup, vampire-like clothing, and devoted herself to very gross and bloody literature. Yet Ana was one of the friendliest, most helpful students in my class. Administrators might include using a checklist or commercial "warning signs list" where administrators check off nonconforming traits of students to see if a threat exists. However, students who pose true threats are often unassuming or may not meet the required "6 out of 10 checkmarks" or whatever the threshold is to warrant an investigation by school administrators. The concept of threat assessment is not a formula or even a profoundly accurate means of identifying a true threat. Former U.S. Attorney General Janet Reno wrote an introduction to the FBI's threat assessment model and stated,

> If we use this threat assessment model judiciously—and we must, because the risk of unfairly labeling and stigmatizing children is great—then we will be able to fight, and win, the war on two fronts. We will be in a position to help those children who show a propensity for violence, before they scare themselves (and others) forever. And we will be in a position to protect innocent school children before they become senseless victims (O'Toole, 2000, p. ii).

Threat assessment involves a thorough investigation within the context of an event as applied to the individuals involved. It does not assume broad generalizations, predict violent behavior, or assure safety. It is one piece of the puzzle to ensuring student safety.

Threat assessment can take many forms, and for the purposes of this text, we will focus only on student violent writing, not on the myriad of other threats that need to be assessed within a school building (armed intruders). Hyman (2006) promoted the idea that schools can create threat assessment procedures that not only investigate the true possibility of a threat but that can also provide feedback on the overall school culture. He listed six principles of the threat assessment process, including the principles that an investigative mindset is "skeptical and inquisitive" and that effective threat assessment is based on facts rather than "traits" (p. 137). An inquisitive threat assessment would look more at the why and how of a situation rather than seeking only punitive measures regardless of motivation.

Dealing with student violent writing calls for use of the "investigative" threat assessment technique where student writing is studied and carefully considered rather than instantly resulting in disciplinary proceedings. This investigation should include an eight-step analysis of the writing and writer that includes:

1. Reading the writing in full (and making a photocopy of the writing)

2. Inquiring with the person who discovered the writing (student, staff member, parent) about the situation surrounding the creation of the writing

3. Thoroughly investigating the disciplinary history of a student

4. Studying the personal profiles of students, including family issues, legal problems, or overall personality issues

5. Personally discussing the writing with the classroom teacher (if the writing was created in a classroom) and reviewing the writing policies of the classroom

6. Noting any school cultural or climate issues that exist in the writing (is the student writing about being bullied or feeling unsupported in the school environment?) and compiling supporting evidence on the existence of these issues

7. Interviewing the student and carefully listening to the student response about the motivation for the writing

8. Consulting available mental health practitioners or law enforcement personnel as needed. It should be noted that if the writing contains a direct threat to harm oneself or others, law enforcement should always be consulted.

Listening and Threat Assessment

School administrators must respond to student violent writing with some sort of interaction with the writer personally, whether it is a formal interview or an informal conversation. It is extremely important for an administrator to be prepared to listen carefully to what the student is saying—not just whether or not he or she admits to writing a piece but why the student wrote the piece and any other pieces that might reveal a truly troubled student. In several cases reviewed for this text, students told various reasons for graphic writings—from "it was a joke" to "I didn't mean anything by it." It is imperative an administrator take such statements into consideration, especially when judging whether a piece of writing is a true threat. After all, a piece of student violent writing where the student defends the piece as "I was modeling what we read in a class novel" may diffuse the overall threat of the piece. In addition, there is always the possibility that a student who has written a violent piece is seeking help and may need some sort of mental health assistance.

Not only should administrators listen to a student's rationale for creating a piece of student violent writing, but they should also be "listening" to the cultural messages sent by society to students today. Russo and Delon (1999b) stated,

> Children today are bombarded with movies, television shows, and music and even news broadcasts that depict and some-times appear to advocate behavior that only a generation ago would have been considered shocking and socially unaccept-able. Often, the language used by television and parroted by teenagers and younger children in everyday conversation goes far beyond that of their "baby-boomer" parents in vul-garity and obscenity (p. 604).

There are some interesting examples of student excuses presented in published case law. In *Lovell v. Poway Unified School District* (1996), a frustrated student threatened to kill a school counselor and later told the school administrator that she was frustrated by some office pro-cedures and that she did not mean what she said. In another case, a student reported his violent writing was "all fiction" and was inspired by an activity his mom was working on in her college level creative writing class. And in one case where a student drew a picture of him-self shooting a police officer, he later reported he did so to express his anger. Students should have the opportunity to be heard and to offer explanations for their writing. With today's students having vast exposure to violent movies, television, and Internet content, it only makes sense that this content bleeds into the content of student writ-ing, both in and out of school. Today's teachers and administrators need to be prepared to listen to student rationale with the possibility the outcome of the conversation will not be disciplinary in nature.

Keep a Copy of Student Writing

At one point in my teaching career my assistant principal told me, "If you don't document something that happens with a student in your classroom, it's like it never happened." Although this is an exaggeration of sorts, administrators should go to great lengths to document each step they make when dealing with student expressive writing that is troublesome; this protects the record for a variety of potential legal appeals. While there is no standard, court-approved documentation form or process, there are several principles that should be adhered to:

- Making copies of student violent writing immediately on receipt of the writing and maintaining the original copy in a safe, secure location. One interesting case out of Kansas dealt with a piece of violent artwork created by a student. The principal made several copies of the artwork but left the original piece lying on his desk. When he stepped out of the office to tend to other matters, the student, who was waiting for him in the principal's office, destroyed the original copy.
- Use the "Sample Threat Assessment Form for Student Violent Writing Incidents" from this chapter and remember to report statements from students and staff members (not just the ones involved but anyone who might have knowledge of the event or the student) and to meticulously detail the thematic problems with the writing.
- Requiring students to sign statements such as "I, Jane Doe, wrote this piece for English class on February 2, 2010." Doing so creates some sort of acknowledgment by the student as well as adding credence to the reliability of the documentation file.

A Sample Threat Assessment Form for Student Violent Writing Incidents

Name: _____

Grade Level: _____

Origination of Writing

- ❏　written at home
- ❏　classroom assignment
- ❏　within a classroom but not part of an assignment
- ❏　on a social networking site
- ❏　communications between students
- ❏　personal diary or journal

Thematic Issues Within the Writing

- ❐ excessive violence
- ❐ graphic description
- ❐ death
- ❐ murder
- ❐ sexual content
- ❐ threats to others
- ❐ threats to self
- ❐ Other (describe)

Questions for the Teacher Interviewee
(or One Who First Gained Knowledge of Student Writing)

- In what context was the writing discovered or created?
- Has the student displayed any other issues within the classroom (for example, disruptive behavior, defiance of authority)?
- How would you describe your relationship with the student?
- Have you discussed the writing with the student?
- What problems do you see within the writing?

Questions for the Student Author

- What was the motivation for the writing?
- Where did you write the piece?
- Why did you write the piece?
- What were you trying to accomplish?
- Can you share more about things you like to write about?
- Do you understand why we might be concerned with your writing?
- Do you need to talk about any problems you are facing?

Questions to Ask Parents or Guardians

- Is the student or family facing any problems?
- Has the student displayed any disturbing behavior at home?
- Is the student suicidal?
- Does the student have access to any weapons?
- Have there been recent mood changes?
- Has the student expressed any concerns about social relationships at issue at school?

Information to Provide to Law Enforcement

Provide law enforcement with a copy of the writing and a summary of all interviews. In addition, provide all pertinent student disciplinary documents that may shed light on the student's mental capacity. Provide contact information for teacher, parents, and all involved administrators.

Summary

Threat assessment must be thorough and carefully executed. While it may seem wise to act swiftly, it is more important to respond carefully. Be prepared to not only read and tend to the details of student violent writing but also to carefully listen to the stories of those involved—the student author, the classroom teacher, and a range of others that might have useful knowledge about the student. Stop for a moment, make and secure a copy of the student writing, and begin to investigate by talking to those closest to the situation and documenting with detail the origination, content, and background of the student writing. The next chapter deals with acting and responding to student violent writing in a timely and thoughtful manner, including reviewing some commonly overlooked details in the documentation process.

Practical Applications for Teachers and Administrators

For K–6 Schools

- Create a form or paper documentation technique for your school to assess a student violent writing threat as a unique event. Use the example provided in this text or consult Cornell and Sheras's text (2006) for guidance to formulate a form that suits your needs.
- Identify ways to track students with potential violence issues that include a student's academic record, information about home life, and behavior patterns. Use this to create a whole picture of a student, not simply to profile potential bad seeds.
- Identify who will handle a threat assessment. Notify these personnel of their specific responsibilities.

- Participate in a tabletop exercise of a student violent writing episode.
- Prepare a method to immediately copy and secure copies of student writing upon receipt.
- Know that dealing with student writing incidents takes time—interviewing, conferencing, and listening. Have someone available to take over for you in your other roles when you need to begin an investigation.
- Inform teachers and parents of the procedure you will go through to assess a student violent writing event. Be open about the process and procedures and also solicit suggestions from these groups.
- Your relationships with students will be important as you conduct a threat assessment. Up to this point you should be visible frequently throughout the building, visiting classes daily, and conversing with students personally often.
- Work with law enforcement specifically on how you will be assessing student violent writing issues before one arises. Identify your personal contact with the local police. Have law enforcement contact information readily available at all times.

For 7–12 Schools

- Identify your threat assessment team and notify these personnel of their specific responsibilities.
- Participate in a tabletop exercise of a student violent writing event.
- Prepare a method to immediately copy and secure copies of student violent writing.
- Identify ways to track students with potential violence issues that include a student's academic record, information about home life, and behavior patterns. Use this to create a whole picture of a student, not simply to profile potential bad seeds.
- Identify who can take over for you when you need to deal with a student violent writing investigation. Be able to trust that person so that you can focus on listening to those involved in the student violent writing event.
- Inform teachers and parents of your threat assessment protocol for student violent writing events. Use this opportunity to discuss the unique nature of student writing and student violent writing events.

- Build rapport with students daily by visiting classrooms, being visible throughout the building, and informally talking to students.
- Work with law enforcement specifically on how you will be assessing student violent writing issues before one arises. Identify your personal contact with the local police. Have law enforcement contact information readily available at all times.

Questions to Consider

1. Do you intentionally or unintentionally profile students? If so, how has that helped or hindered your student relationships?

2. What are your worst fears about threat assessment? How can you address these now as a preventative measure?

3. How can you build stronger connections with outside resources, such as law enforcement personnel and counseling services?

4. How do you convey to parents and students that you are prepared to handle a threat assessment protocol?

9

Acting and Responding to Student Violent Writing

Exercise those plans. Don't put them on a shelf and let them collect dust. When the crisis happens, that's not the time to figure out all the details.
—Gregory A. White, U.S. Attorney, Northern District of Ohio

The Need for a Timely Response

Teachers and administrators need to respond in a timely fashion when dealing with student violent writing. It may seem like an obvious point, but several court cases dealing with student violent writing painted pictures of administrators who simply were not punctual in their response times and in turn left an entire student body at risk. Consider these scenarios:

- In *D.G. v. Tulsa* (2000), a student wrote a poem threatening to kill her teacher after a run-in with the teacher. The poem was tossed on the floor and later turned in to the school's assistant principal. The assistant principal contacted the student *six days* after first receiving the poem, conferenced with the student, and then returned the student to class. Then, the assistant principal contacted the student's parents and informed them that the student was being suspended for violating the school's policy forbidding threats against other students.

- In *Lovell v. Poway Unified School District* (1996), after a tiresome day of attempting to change her class schedule, a student threatened to kill a school counselor out of exasperation. The counselor reported the threat to the principal the same day. It was not until two days later that the assistant principal met with the student to discuss the situation and initiate the student's suspension.

- In *Ponce v. Socorro Independent School District* (2007), a student was suspended based on the content of a diary he had written. After interviewing the student and hearing the student's claims that the violent depictions in his writing were "all fiction," the assistant principal sent the student back to class. The assistant principal took the diary home overnight and after a more thorough reading determined the student was a danger to other students. It was then, after having initially been returned to class, that the student was suspended for three days.

- In *Demers v.* Leominster *School Department* (2003), as well, a student who wrote "I hate life" and "I want to die" did not initially meet with the school principal until the day after the school principal received the writing.

It is simply neither sound nor safe practice to return a student who has written or voiced some violent content or intent back to the general student population before an investigation takes place. Questions could be raised about (a) how real or imminent the threat was if the student was returned to class after the administrative interview and then later suspended for being a threat, (b) how serious the threat was based on the time lapse between the administrator receiving the piece of writing and the initial conference with the student, and (c) whether the best interest of the student body was first and foremost if a delay occurred before the student was contacted about a violent or suicidal piece of writing. In all four cases illustrated previously, administrators seemed to be lagging in their responses when they returned students to class and then later suspended the same student as a threat. Lapse of time poses two problems. First, the administrator may be returning a truly violent student to the classroom, and second, the administrator appears disorganized or unable to make sound decisions at a crucial time. Administrators need to make acting timely a top priority—to determine if a student is indeed a threat and should or should not be returned to the classroom. Seek an alternative placement, even temporarily, including having the student meet with a counselor, serve an in-school suspension, or simply sitting with an administrator to complete coursework while the situation can be investigated. Reading a piece of student violent writing and acting immediately demonstrates the urgent and important priority of protecting the school population while protecting student Constitutional rights.

Responding Reasonably to All Student Violent Writing

All student violent writing will require some type of response, from a brief investigation by a classroom teacher to a thorough review by law enforcement personnel. Each response will be different and unpredictable. However, every incident of student violent writing should result in action by teachers and school administrators. Virginia school superintendent Mark Lineburg reiterated the importance of a response (as opposed to a scripted school response) by stating,

> We [as a school] are going to take action. Action does NOT mean suspension or discipline. We are going to conference, call parents, prepare documentation, dialogue with each other . . . we are not going to sit back and do nothing. We are going to protect our institution from being liable for student violence and we are going to protect our students at all costs (M. Lineburg, personal communication, January 10, 2012).

Sometimes student violent writing may require contacting law enforcement personnel, most notably when the writing threatens direct harm to oneself or others. It is best in these circumstances to have a protocol set in place, even among the administrative team in your school, as to when law enforcement will be contacted, who will contact them, and how the school will work in conjunction with them. Having a written plan already in place will help eliminate confusion and missing elements to creating a fully informed report to law enforcement. Many schools today utilize school resource officers or in-house police officers and this may eliminate the need for a formal call to outside law enforcement. It is important that administrators stay abreast of current local, state, and federal laws that might impact reporting requirements for student violent writing. Do not hesitate to contact a colleague, school attorney, or other informed source to help talk through a school legal issue.

Creating a Documentation Trail

There is no one tried and true method of documenting student violent writing incidents. The Virginia Tech English Department drafted a set of guidelines as an internal document that illustrates some interesting questions administrators can consider about the content of student writing, including inquiring as to whether the writing was inspired by a favorite horror writer or whether the writing was the first piece of violent writing submitted by a student. (See Cornell and Sheras's Guidelines for Responding to Student Threats of Violence, 2006.)

The previous chapter included a protocol of qualities of the violent writing, questions to ask when discussing the writing with the student, and suggestions for follow-up responses. This checklist can be adapted or refined to fit the individual needs of your school, but the idea remains the same. It is important to document the type of writing, the occasion of the writing, and any other sort of behavior that might help paint a full picture of the student's overall disciplinary issues. It is imperative to retell the involved staff and student statements in an almost verbatim fashion. The most important piece is that documentation is thorough, accurate, and secure. You should maintain control of the documentation at all times. At some point you may be asked to reproduce your documentation rather quickly for law enforcement personnel so it is imperative that you have immediate access and a thorough record on which to rely.

Potential Administrative Responses

It is generally agreed that a zero tolerance, immediate expulsion approach to student violent writing is not helpful to anyone—the student is not afforded ample opportunity to explain or counsel through the violent writing situation and the school has not done an adequate job of teaching the lessons of purpose and responsibility in writing. Several disciplinary options should be considered when a student is determined to not be a true threat to the learning environment:

1. A participatory conference with the student's parents or guardians and the student to discuss the nature of the writing and the problem with the writing within the school setting. In this conference, create an action or behavior plan, generated by the entire group, for dealing with future similar incidents involving this student.

2. Required follow-up instruction from the classroom teacher—perhaps the student needs time to talk through appropriate writing responses with the writing professional. Arrange for this to happen and provide the necessary instructional materials.

3. Required meetings with school counselors. Meeting with a school counselor can be as frequent or infrequent as needed or determined necessary. This path, however, provides the student a person to connect with and with whom to build a relationship. Even though this may be time consuming for a student, it should be seen as a positive culture builder.

4. Follow-up conferences with the assigned administrator, again to build a relationship and act as a support within the school building.

5. Conflict resolution sessions. Especially in the elementary grades but also in the tumultuous years of adolescence, conflict resolution strategies may be a good solution, particularly if the student violent writing was the result of a poor school climate or a negative school culture. These types of programs might involve some peer counseling, some conflict resolution skill training sessions, some walk-through dramatic episodes, or some brainstorming sessions.

6. Rewriting. Allowing the student the opportunity to revisit the writing that caused this issue might allow the student to view the writing in a new light, especially after an administrative intervention. By allowing the student to review the work and redraft the content, the student is given a chance to practice the skill with a heightened awareness for the problems some violent writing can create.

Alternative administrative responses to student violent writing incidents

- Conferences with parents and counselors
- Required re-teaching by classroom writing teacher
- Recurrent follow-up conferences to encourage relationships building and accountability
- Mandatory conflict resolution sessions
- Allowing student to rewrite the problem piece of writing

Summary

School administrators must respond to all student violent writing. When a student authors a piece of violent writing, the student should be removed from the student population until a threat assessment can be completed. In addition, responding to student violent writing should be reasonable and not overreaching or overly punitive. Realize that students, in their youth, make mistakes and exercise poor judgment. Be willing to find alternative responses to student violent writing incidents that are not necessarily disciplinary in nature. While it is important to respond in some fashion to all student violent writing, be confident that your response is thoughtful and applicable to the individual student whom you are educating.

Practical Applications for Teachers and Administrators

For K–6 Schools

- Identify the response options for student violent writings that do not include suspension or expulsion. Make a list and keep it handy for easy reference when you need ideas on other options for behavior interventions.
- Prepare a desk or work area in the school office where a student can complete school work or remain out of class while an investigation occurs and the student cannot be returned to class. Have some age-appropriate materials available for the student to work on while passing time if necessary (novels or workbooks should suffice).
- Identify who is responding to student violent writing and what his or her specific role will be. Be sure to include alternatives in case someone is absent on the day a threat assessment is needed.
- Contact parents immediately when you remove a student for a student violent writing incident—if for no other reason than to inform the parent of the student's temporary alternative placement.
- Be prepared with follow-up activities. Have forms prepared for a behavior plan, a conference log, or a conflict resolution plan.
- Be prepared to decipher what information needs to be shared with staff after a student violent writing incident. In addition,

if a viable threat was made, communicate minimal and necessary information to parents (as directed by law enforcement) emphasizing your efforts to ensure school safety.

For 7–12 Schools

- Identify alternative consequences for negative student behavior that do not include suspension or expulsion. Keep this list handy for ideas when you need some options.
- Draft a student violent writing incident form that is compliant with your school district's policies. Make multiple copies, share with your staff, and keep handy.
- Prepare a desk or work area in the school office where a student who has been removed from class because of student violent writing can work. This area should be monitored at all times.
- Confiscate all student communication devices (cell phone, laptops) so that the student cannot communicate with students who may still be in class.
- Contact parents immediately before you begin an investigation on student violent writing—if for no other reason than to inform the parents of the student's removal from class.
- Be prepared to decipher what information needs to be shared with staff after a student violent writing incident. In addition, if a viable threat was made, communicate minimal and necessary information to parents (as directed by law enforcement) emphasizing your efforts to ensure school safety.

Questions to Consider

1. Are you emotionally prepared to respond to a student violent writing incident? Who do you trust to help you through these events?

2. How will you decide what information to share with staff and parents, many of whom will press you for information you may be unable or unwilling to share?

3. How do you communicate your school safety priorities to your constituents?

4. How can you determine appropriate alternative disciplinary techniques on a student-by-student basis? Where can you learn more about these techniques?

Appendix

Proposed Threat Assessment From Dr. Lori Brown's Dissertation (2011)

Procedures for Addressing Violent Writing

1. School system designates a threat assessment coordinator.

2. Threat assessment coordinator is well trained to recognize FBI identified warning signs of threats, including behavioral, written, or verbal threats.

3. Coordinator prepares a training plan for the school system. The plan should adopt a train-the-trainer model with school-based counselors, social workers, and administrators trained in the district's comprehensive approach to school threat assessment. These school staff members in turn train school-based instructional and non-instructional staff. District training plan must involve specific attention to specialized training for English/ELA teachers.

4. Coordinator is trained to recognize the categories of the researcher's violent writing typology, to identify those requiring the most immediate attention, and to determine appropriate responses to each category. (Example: Direct threat writings

must be submitted immediately to the principal. Fantasy violence with indirect threats and self-inflicted violent writing, especially suicidal writings, should be submitted to the school counselor or other school-based mental health staff who have been trained by the district coordinator in threat assessment procedures. Other categorical responses may vary).

5. Coordinator trains all school-based English and English Language Arts instructors in the violent writing typology and associated recommended response, with emphasis on the idea that even violent writings can be and most often are innocuous. Teacher training supports the idea that teachers alone should not determine a student's potential threat level. Instead, they need to understand the role of school point persons in helping them determine potential levels of threat/risk. A half-day (3 hours) of training with specific writing examples and possible classroom scenarios is recommended.

6. With the exception of direct threat violent writing, classroom teachers are instructed to first address violent texts informally with the student. The purpose of this discussion is to make an initial determination about student intent and to provide information to the threat assessment point persons who become involved in the process. This recommendation follows Virginia Tech's approach to disturbing creative writing.

7. After discussion with the student, the teacher determines to make no further response, or to pursue a school-based threat and risk assessment process with the school point person. This process must involve communication with the parents and the student's other teachers.

8. The school-based threat assessment point person works with the district coordinator or district threat assessment staff to conduct an appropriate threat/risk assessment.

9. Results of assessment are shared with teacher, student, parent, etc., and proper responses given. The process for determining the threat level of violent writing should mirror the process used with violent or disturbing behaviors among youth.

10. Combined with attention to faculty/staff training, students and their parents must be made aware of the above-recommended process for potential student threats, a recommendation emphasized by the FBI (O'Toole, 2000).

References and Further Reading

42 U.S.C. §1983 (2000).

100 most frequently challenged books 1990–2000. (n.d.). Retrieved from http://ala8.ala.org/ala/oif/bannedbooksweek/bbwlinks/100mostfrequently.htm

Atkinson, A. J. (2005). *Zero tolerance policies: An issue brief.* Retrieved from http://doe.virginia.gov/VDOE/suptsmemos/2006/inf003a.pdf

Attorney: Teen who wrote violent essay is returning to school. (2007, May 7). *Associated Press.* Retrieved on September 25, 2008, from http://www.firstamendmentcenter.org/attorney-teen-who-wrote-violent-essay-is-returning-to-school

Bethel School District No. 403 v. Fraser, 478 U.S. 675. (1986).

Beussink v. Woodland R-IV School District, 30 F. Supp. 2d 1175 (E.D. Mo. 1998).

Blystone, R. V. (2007). School speech v. school safety: In the aftermath of violence on school campuses throughout this nation, how should school officials respond to threatening student expression? *BYU Education and Law Journal,* 199.

Boim v. Fulton County School District, 494 F.3d 978 (11th Cir. 2007).

Boman v. Bluestem Unified School Disrict No. 205, 2000 U.S. Dist. LEXIS 5389. (2000).

Boston schools drop suspension of chain-saw storyteller. (2000, May 18). *Associated Press.* Retrieved from http://www.freedomforum.org/templates/document.asp?documentID=12497

Brooke, J. (1999, May 11). Teacher of Colorado gunmen alerted parents. *New York Times.*

Brown, L. (2011). *Violent writing: A quantitative examination of an unexploded high school phenomenon* (Doctoral dissertation). Retrieved from ProQuest (UMI 3460881).

Burke, J. (2003). *The English teacher's companion: A complete guide to classroom, curriculum, and the profession.* Portsmouth, NH: Heinemann.

Calvert, C., & Richards, R. D. (2003). Columbine fallout: The long-term effects on free expression take hold in public schools. *Boston University Law Review, 83,* 1089.

Carrier v. Lake Pend School District #84, 134 P.3d 655 (Idaho 2006).

Chalmers, P. (2011). *Inside the mind of a teen killer.* Nashville, TN: Thomas Nelson.

Cornell, D. & Sheras, P. (2006). *Guidelines for responding to student threats of violence.* Longmont, CO: Sopris West.

Couvillon, M. A., & Ilieva, V. (2011). Recommended practices: A review of schoolwide preventative programs and strategies on cyberbullying. *Preventing School Failure, 55*(2), 96-101. doi:10.1080/1045988X.2011.539461

Cuff v. Valley Central School District, 559 F. Supp. 2d 415 (N.Y. 2008).

Cullen, D. (2009). *Columbine.* New York, NY: Twelve—Hachette Book Group.

Deal, T. E., & Peterson, K. D. (1999). *Shaping school culture: The heart of leadership.* San Francisco, CA: Jossey-Bass.

Demers v. Leominster School Department, 263 F. Supp. 2d 195 (D. Mass. 2003).

D. G. v. Independent School District #11 of Tulsa County Oklahoma, 2000 U.S. Dist. LEXIS 12197. (2000, August 21).

D. J. M. v. Hannibal Public School District No. 60, 647 F.3d 754 (8th Cir. 2011).

Doe v. Pulaski County Special School District, 306 F.3d 616 (2002).

Doninger v. Niehoff, 527 F. 3d 41 (2008).

Fein, R. A., Vossekuil, B., Pollack, W., Borum, R., Modzeleski, W., & Reddy, M. (2002). *Threat assessment in the schools: A guide to managing threatening situations and to creating safe school climates.* Washington, DC: U.S. Department of Education and U.S. Secret Service.

Grunbaum, J., Kann, L., Kinchen, S., Ross, J., Hawkins, J., Lowry, R., . . . Collins, J. (2004). Youth risk behavior surveillance—United States, 2003 (Abridged). *Journal of School Health, 74*(8), 307–324.

Hazelwood School District v. Kuhlmeier, 484 U.S. 260. (1988).

Heard, K. (1999). Killer's essay haunts Westside teacher. *Arkansas Democrat Gazette.* Retrieved from http://www.arkansasonline.com

Hoover, J. H., & Oliver, R. (1996). *The bullying prevention handbook: A guide for principals, teachers, and counselors.* Bloomington, IN: National Education Service.

Hyman, R. T. (2006). *Death threats by students: The law and its implications.* Dayton, OH: Education Law Association.

In his own words: Cary-Grove teen's musings. (2007, April 28). *Chicago Tribune.* Retrieved from http://articles.chicagotribune.com/2007–04–28/news/0704271261_1_obscenity-stab-teacher

Ingold, J., & Pankratz, H. (2003, January 9). Columbine killers left paper trail: Violent writings by killers released with horrific details of massacre. *The Denver Post*, pp. A-01.

Jefferson County Public Schools Board Policy. (2012). Retrieved from http://www.jeffcopublicschools.org/board/

Jimerson, S. R., Brock, S. E., Greif, J. L., & Cowan, K. C. (2004). *Threat assessment at school: A primer for educators.* Bethesda, MD: National Association of School Psychologists.

Jones v. Arkansas, 64 S.W.3d 728 (Ark. 2002).

Jossey-Bass Inc. (2001). *The Jossey-Bass reader on educational leadership.* San Francisco, CA: Jossey-Bass.

J. S. v. Bethlehem Area School District, 569 Pa. 638 (2002).

J. S. v. Blue Mountain School District, 593 F.3d 286 (3d Cir. 2010).

Kansas City Public Schools Student Code of Conduct. (2012). Retrieved from http://kckps.org/code/

King, S. (2007, April 23). On predicting violence. *Entertainment Weekly.* Retrieved from http://www.ew.com/ew/article/0,,20036014,00.html

Kowalski v. Berkeley County Schools, 652 F.3d 565 (4th Cir. 2011).

Kupchik, A. (2010). *Homeroom security.* New York: New York University Press.

Layshock v. Hermitage School District, 496 F. Supp. 2d 587, 596–597 (W.D. Pa. 2007).

Lincoln Public Schools Board Policy. (2008). Retrieved from http://www .lps.org

Lovell v. Poway Unified School District, 90 F.3d 367 (9th Cir. 1996).

Macrorie, K. (1985). *Telling writing* (4th ed.). Portsmouth, NH: Boynton/ Cook.

Morse v. Frederick, 127 S. Ct. 2618. (2007).

National Center for Education Statistics, U.S. Department of Education. (2007). *Indicators of school crime and safety: 2007.* Retrieved from http://bjs. ojp.usdoj.gov/index.cfm?ty=pbdetail&iid=1762

National School Boards Association. (2011). *Students on board: A conversation between school board members and students* [Brochure]. Retrieved from http://www.pearsonfoundation.org/pr/20110810-NSBA-Launches-Board-Student-Conversations.html

Nelson, G. L. (2000). Warriors with words: Toward a post-Columbine writing curriculum. *English Journal, 89*(5), 42–46.

New York City Department of Education Discipline Code. (2011). Retrieved from http://schools.nyc.gov/RulesPolicies/DisciplineCode/default .htm

Obama, B. (2011, July 18). Staying competitive through education: The President and American business leaders announce new commitments [Web log post]. Retrieved from http://www.whitehouse.gov/ blog/2011/07/18/staying-competitive-through-education-president-and-american-business-leaders-announ

Oltman, G. (2009). *Dealing with student violent writing in the English classroom: A framework for public school administrators.* Ph.D. dissertation, The University of Nebraska—Lincoln, United States—Nebraska. Retrieved May 20, 2012 from Dissertations & Theses @ University of Nebraska -Lincoln. (Publication No. AAT 3350257).

Osborne, A. G., & Russo, C. J. (in press). Can students be disciplined for off-campus cyberspeech: The reach of the First Amendment in the age of technology. *Brigham Young University Education and Law Journal.*

O'Toole, M. E. (2000). *The school shooter: A threat assessment perspective.* Quantico, VA: National Center for the Analysis of Violent Crime, Federal Bureau of Investigation.

Peterson, R. L., & Schoonover, B. (2008). *Fact sheet #3: Zero tolerance policies in schools.* Retrieved from http://www.preventschoolviolence.org

Ponce v. Socorro Independent School District, No. 06–50709 (5th Cir. Nov. 20, 2007).

Redfield, S. (2003). Threats made, threats posed: School and judicial analysis in need of redirection. *BYU Education and Law Journal,* 663.

Rhode Island school settles lawsuit brought by student suspended for essay. (2001). *Associated Press.* Retrieved from: http://www.firstamendmentcenter.org/r-i-school-settles-lawsuit-brought-by-student-suspended-for-essay

Russo, C. J., & Delon, F. G. (1999b). Warning: Student expressive activities and assignments may be hazardous to their teachers' employment health. *Education Law Reporter, 132*(3), 595.

Salazar, P. (2008). *High-impact leadership for high-impact schools: The actions that matter most.* Larchmont, NY: Eye on Education.

Schaps, E., & Lewis, C. C. (1998). Breeding citizenship through community in school. *Education Digest, 64*(1), 23.

"School principal cyberbullied with raunchy Facebook page." Retrieved from http://www.kirotv.com/news/news/school-principal-cyberbullied-with-raunchy-faceboo/nD6HF/

Schoonover, J. (2007). The application, consequences, and alternatives to zero tolerance policies in Florida schools. *Proceedings of Persistently Safe Schools, USA,* 231–241.

Secret service investigates 7th-grader's violent essay. (2006, February 4). *Associated Press.* Retrieved from http://www.firstamendmentcenter.org//news.aspx?id+16423&SearchString=westwarwick

Secret service questions student about anti-war drawings. (2004, April 27). *Associated Press.* Retrieved from http://www.firstamendmentcenter.org//news.aspx?id=13245&SearchString=prosser

Shelton v. Tucker, 364 U.S. 479, 487 (1960).

Skiba, R. J. (2000). Zero tolerance, zero evidence: An analysis of school disciplinary practice. Retrieved from http://www.indiana.edu/~safeschl/publication.html

Slonje, R., & Smith, P. K. (2008), Cyberbullying: Another main type of bullying? *Scandinavian Journal of Psychology, 49,* 147–154.

Swedberg, N., & Olson, E. R. (2007, April 26). Disturbing essay details revealed. *Northwest Herald.* Retrieved from http://nl.newsbank.com/nl-search/we/Archives?p_multi=NWRB&p_product=SHNP8&p_theme=shnp8&p_action=search&p_maxdocs=200&p_field_label-0=title&p_text_label-0=Disturbing%20essay%20details%20revealed&s_dispstring=headline%28Disturbing%20essay%20details%20revealed%29&xcal_numdocs=20&p_perpage=10&p_sort=YMD_date:D&xcal_useweights=no

Tchudi, S. J., & Tchudi, S. (1999). *The English language arts handbook: Classroom strategies for teachers*. Portsmouth, NH: Boynton/Cook.

"The letter police said Chandler students wrote about killing their teacher." (2012). Retrieved from: http://www.azcentral.com/community/chandler/articles/2011/11/10/20111110chandler-teacher-threatened-death1110.html

Tinker v. Des Moines Independent School District, 393 U.S. 503. (1969).

Uerling, D. F. (1999). Schooling for character and citizenship: Legal grounds for pursuing educational goals. In S. Stick (Ed.), *Foundations of modern education* (pp. A-5 to A-10). Boston, MA: Pearson Custom.

U.S. Const. amend. I

USA school violence statistics. (n.d.). Retrieved on September 22, 2008, from http://www.cybersnitch.net/schoolwatchs/svstats.asp#1992

West Virginia Board of Education v. Barnette, 319 U.S. 624 (1943).

Whitaker, T. (2003). *What great principals do differently*. Larchmont, NY: Eye on Education.

Index

American Bar Association, 45

American Library Association, 56

Angelou, M., 23

Anger problems
  case law on student violence related
    to, 33
  as indicator of potential violence, 54

Antiviolence writing programs, 55–56

Aristotle, 23

Arkansas, Jones v., 33

Arkansas school shooting, 1

Atkinson, A. J., 44

Authority problems, 33

Baluvelt, P., 45

*Barnette, West Virginia Board of
    Education v.,* 11

Being snubbed, 33

Berkeley County Schools, Kowalski v., 64

Bethel School District No. 403 v. Fraser,
    15–16, 19, 20, 24–25, 26, 46, 65

Bethlehem Area School District, J.S. v., 5

*Beussink v. Woodland R-IV School
    District,* 33

"Blood, Sex, and Booze" (student
    story), 7, 53

Blue Mountain, J.S. v., 67

*Bluestem Unified School District,
    Boman v.,* 33

Blystone, R. V., 57

Boim v. Fulton County School District, 33

*Boman v. Bluestem Unified School
    District,* 33

"BONG HiTS 4JESUS" banner
    case, 18

Boston Schools Drop, 6

Boyfriend/girlfriend problems, 33,
    64–65

Boys Town Education Model, 23

Brock, S. E., 82

Brooke, J., 4

Brown, L., 77, 83

Bullying
  case law related to violence response
    to, 33
  complaints by Columbine shooters on
    being, 32
  Gun-Free Schools Act (1994) to
    combat, 44
  as indicator of potential violence, 54
  school survey on student threat of
    physical attacks and, 2
  See also Cyberbullying

Burke, J., 56–57, 74, 76

Bush, L., 31

Calvert, C., 5, 6

Carithers, C. (student), 6

*Carrier v. Lake Pend School District
    #84,* 33

Case law
  Bethel v. Fraser, 15–16, 19, 20, 24–25,
    26, 46, 65
  *Beussink v. Woodland R-IV School
    District,* 33
  *Boim v. Fulton County School
    District,* 33
  *Boman v. Bluestem Unified School
    District,* 33
  Carrier v. Lake Pend School District #84, 33
  Cuff v. Valley Central School District, 33
  *Demers v. Leominister School
    Department,* 94
  *D.G. v. Independent School District #11
    of Tulsa County Oklahoma,* 33,
    93–94
  *D.J.M. v. Hannibal Pub. School
    District,* 64

Doe v. Pulaski County Special School District, 64–65
Doninger v. Nyhoff, 65
Hazelwood v. Kuhlmeier, 16–18, 19, 20, 25, 26, 46
Jones v. Arkansas, 33
J.S. v. Bethlehem Area School District, 5
J.S. v. Blue Mountain, 67
Kowalski v. Berkeley County Schools, 64
Layshock v. Hermitage School District, 67
Lovell v. Poway Unified School District, 86, 94
Morse v. Frederick, 18, 20, 25, 26, 46
Ponce v. Socorro Independent School District, 94
Shelton v. Tucker, 24
Tinker v. Des Moines Independent School District, 13–15, 24, 25, 26, 46, 64, 65, 69
West Virginia Board of Education v. Barnette, 11
See also Schools; U.S. Supreme Court
Cavett, D., 43
Censoring student writing
debate over classroom writing and, 57–58
Fraser decision on vulgar or offensive speech, 15–16, 19, 20, 24–25, 26, 46
Hazelwood decision on "basic educational mission" inconsistency and, 16–18, 19, 20, 25, 26, 46
Morse decision on promoting illegal drug use, 18, 20, 25, 26, 46
Tinker standard to assess writing for, 14–15, 19–20, 24, 26, 46, 64, 65, 69
true threat standard to assess for, 20–21
Chalmers, P., 54
Character Counts program, 23
Citizenship education
through the curriculum, 22–24
debate over whose values to teach in, 21–22
practical applications on teaching, 27–29
public schools charge with providing, 21, 26–27
selected programs for, 23
Civil Rights Act (1871), 12–13
Clinton, B., 1
Columbine effect
practical applications for teachers and administrators, 8–9

questions to consider related to the, 9–10
on school administrators, 5–6
on the student writers, 6–8
"Columbine fallout: The long-term effects on free expression take hold in public schools" (Calvert & Richards), 6
Columbine school shooting (1999)
character and writings by the two shooters in, 3–4, 32
Clinton's address following the, 1
plea to prevent violence through writing after the, 55
Rachel's Challenge program named after first victim in, 23
shock and images of the, 2–3
Community impact, 9
"Confidentiality" classroom policies, 75, 76
Conflict resolution sessions, 97
Consortium to Prevent School Violence, 45
Cornell, D, 83, 89
COSA Twitter feed, 69
Council of School Attorneys (COSA), 69
Couvillon, M. A., 66
Cowan, K. C., 82
Creative writing. *See* Writing classroom
Cuff v. Valley Central School District, 33
Cullen, D., 33, 37
Cyberbullying
administrator and teacher applications for prevention of, 70–71
case law decisions on, 64–66
description and discipline of, 66–67
schoolwide prevention programs to stop, 66–67
See also Bullying

Deal, T. E., 31, 32, 37
Declaration of Independence, 27
Delon, F. G., 86
Demers v. Leominister School Department, 94
Depression, 54
Des Moines Independent School District, Tinker v., 13–15, 24, 26, 46, 64, 65, 69
Dewey, J., 73
D.G. v. Independent School District #11 of Tulsa County Oklahoma, 33, 93–94
Disciplinary actions

"Blood, Sex, and Booze" story leading
    to student arrest, 7
Columbine effect on First Amendment
    rights and, 5–6
conflict resolution sessions, 97
expulsion, 5–6, 43–45
follow-up conferences with assigned
    administrator, 97
legal primer for, 11–29
participatory conference with parents
    and students, 96
required follow-up instruction from
    teacher, 97
required meetings with school
    counselors, 97
rewriting assignments given to
    students, 97
U.S. Secret Service investigations as, 7
See also Schools; Student suspension;
    Students
Disruptive student speech, 15–16
Dissent with authority, 33
*D.J.M. v. Hannibal Pub. School
    District,* 64
*Doe v. Pulaski County Special School
    District,* 64–65
Doninger v. Nyhoff, 65

Education Law Association, 69
ELA Notes, 69
Endorf, D., 59
*The English Language Arts Handbook:
    Classroom Strategies for Teachers*
    (Tchudi & Tchudi), 53–54
"Existences: A Virtual Book" (Klebold,
    Columbine school shooter), 3
Expulsion. *See* Student expulsion

Facebook, 66–67
Federal Bureau of Investigation (FBI)
    Threat Assessment model set forth by
        the, 81–82, 84
    traits that are indicators of violence list
        of the, 54–55
Feeling wrongly accused, 33
Fein, R. A., 2, 36, 83
First Amendment
    Bethel v. Fraser on, 15–16, 19, 20, 24–25,
        26, 46, 65
    Columbine effects on student rights
        under, 5
    "Columbine fallout:" (Calvert &
        Richards) on student rights
        under, 6

D.J.M. v. Hannibal Pub. School on
    student threat not protected
    by, 64
Doe v. Pulask on student threat not
    protected by, 64–65
Doninger v. Nyhoff decision on
    disruptive online student
    comments, 65
freedom of expression under the, 12, 13
Hazelwood School District v. Kuhlmeier
    on, 16–18, 19, 20, 25, 26, 46
Morse v. Frederick, 18, 20, 25, 26, 46
Tinker standard to assess student
    writing under, 14–15, 19–20, 24,
    26, 46, 64, 65, 69
tips on teaching students about rights
    under the, 27–29
See also Freedom of expression; U.S.
    Constitution
Fraser, Bethel School District No. 403 v.,
    15–16, 19, 20, 24–25, 26, 46, 65
Fraser, M., 15–16
Frederick, Morse v., 18, 20, 25, 26, 46
Freedom of expression
    citizenship education for
        understanding, 21–25
    Civil Rights Act (1871) on, 12–13
    Fourteenth Amendment on, 12, 14
    Fraser decision on vulgar or offensive
        student speech, 15–16, 19, 20,
        24–25, 26, 46
    Hazelwood decision on student speech
        inconsistent with "basic
        educational mission," 16–18, 19,
        20, 25, 26, 46
    legal application to classroom writing
        samples, 19–20
    legal primer for today's public schools,
        11–12
    Morse decision on speech promoting of
        illegal drug use, 18, 20, 25, 26, 46
    staying informed on social and legal
        issues of, 68–69
    Tinker standard for assessing, 13–15,
        19–20, 24, 26, 46, 64, 65, 69
    true threat standard to assess
        threatening speech, 20–21
    See also First Amendment
Freewriting
    description and examples of, 52
    effective use as teaching tool, 53–54
    purpose and audience focus of
        teaching, 54
Fulton County School District, Boim v., 33

Girlfriend/boyfriend problems, 33, 64–65

Golden, Andrew (Jonesboro shooter), 4

Greif, J. L., 82

Grunbaum, J., 2

Gun-Free Schools Act (1994), 44

Hannibal Pub. School District, D.J.M. v., 64

Harris, E. (Columbine shooter)
    actions during Columbine shooting by, 2
    complaints about treatment by other students by, 32
    concerns over graphic violent writing by, 3–4
    "Is Murder or Breaking the Law Ever Justified?" written by, 3
    positive responses by teachers to writing of, 3, 4

Hazelwood School District v. Kuhlmeier, 16–18, 19, 20, 25, 26, 46

Heard, K., 4

Hermitage School District, Layshock v., 67

"High-impact school leader," 36

Homeroom Security (Kupchik), 35–36

Hoover, J. H., 34

Huckleberry Finn (Twain), 56

Hyman, R. T., 84

Ilieva, V., 66

Illegal drug use promotion, 18

Independent School District #11 of Tulsa County Oklahoma, D.G. v., 33

Ingold, J., 4

Inside the Mind of a Teen Killer (Chalmers), 54

"Is Murder or Breaking the Law Ever Justified?" (Harris, Columbine shooter), 3

Jefferson County Public Schools (Colorado), 46

Jimerson, S. R., 82

Johnson, M. (Jonesboro shooter), 4

Jones v. Arkansas, 33

Jonesboro school shooting, 1, 4

Jossey-Bass Educational Leadership Reader, 37

Journal writing
    "confidentiality" classroom policies for, 75, 76
    "Do not read" portion within classroom-written, 60

policies on off-limits topics for, 59–60
    therapeutic benefits of, 55–56

J.S. v. Bethlehem Area School District, 5

J.S. v. Blue Mountain, 67

Kansas City Public Schools (Missouri), 47

Kelly, J., 3

King, S., 57–58, 60

Kipling, R., 51

Klebold, D. (Columbine shooter)
    actions during Columbine shooting by, 2
    complaints about treatment by other students by, 32
    concerns over graphic violent writing by, 3, 4
    "Existences: A Virtual Book" written by, 3
    positive responses by teachers to writing of, 4

Kowalski v. Berkeley County Schools, 64

Kuhlmeier, Hazelwood School District v., 16–18, 19, 20, 25, 26, 46

Kupchik, A., 35–36

Lake Pend School District #84, Carrier v., 33

Layshock v. Hermitage School District, 67

Lee, C., 53

Leominister School Department, Demers v., 94

Lewis, C. C., 22

Lincoln Public Schools (Nebraska), 47

Lineburg, M., 38, 95

Lovell v. Poway Unified School District, 86, 94

Macrorie, K., 53

Mahoney, D., 63

Manson, C., 4

Morse v. Frederick, 18, 20, 25, 26, 46

MySpace
    J.S. v. Blue Mountain on principal parody page, 65
    Kowalski decision on derogatory posting on, 64
    Layshock decision on principal parody page, 65

National Alliance for Safe Schools (NASS), 45

National Association of Secondary School Principals, 45

National Center for Education Statistics, 2
National Council of Teachers of English (NCTE), 75
National School Boards Association, 35
Natural Born Killers (film), 4
Nelson, G. L., 55
New York City Department of Education, 47
Nightingale, F., 23
No Child Left Behind Act (2001), 22
Niehoff, Doninger v., 65

Obama, B., 22
Of Mice and Men (Steinbeck), 56
Off-campus writings
  being prepared to deal with, 63–64
  cases where schools prevailed, 64–65
  cases where students prevailed, 65–66
  cyberbullying, texting, and Facebook, 66–67
  practical applications for teachers and administrators, 70–71
  staying informed on social and legal issues of, 68–69
  when teacher or administrator is targeted by, 67–68
Offensive student speech
  Fraser decision on, 15–16, 19, 20, 24–25, 26, 46
  targeting teachers and administrators, 67–68
Oliver, R., 34
"100 Most Frequently Most Challenged Books" list, 56
O'Toole, M. E., 34, 81

Pankratz, H., 4
Parent, M. (student), 7–8
Parents
  participatory conference with students and, 96
  school communication about violence to, 10
  survey (2004) on support toward zero tolerance policy, 44
  Threat Assessment Form for Student Violent Writing Incidents questions for, 88
"Perfect day" assignment, 7
"Personal-use only" policies, 75
Peterson, K. D., 31, 32, 37
Peterson, R. L., 45

Pet's death, 33
Pledge of Allegiance, 27
Ponce v. Socorro Independent School District, 94
Poway Unified School District, Lovell v., 86, 94
Principal. *See* School administrators
Private violent thoughts, 33
Professional Learning Community (PLC) meetings, 78
Public Agenda survey (2004), 44
Pulaski County Special School District, Doe v., 64–65

Rachel's Challenge program, 23
Redfield, S., 82
Reno, J., 84
Responses to violent writing
  applications for teachers and administrators, 98–99
  creating documentation trail, 96
  need for timely response to violent writing, 93–95
  options for disciplinary actions, 96–97
  reasonable responses to all student violent writing, 95
Rewriting assignments, 97
Rhoade Island School Settles (2001), 8
Richards, R. D., 5, 6
Russo, C. J., 86

Sadness, 33
Safety. *See* Student safety
Salazar, P., 36
Salon (online magazine), 32
Schaps, E., 22
School administrators
  case law decisions on MySpace parody page on, 65
  characteristics of effective principals, 35
  the Columbine effect on, 5–6
  Columbine effect and practical applications for, 8–9
  conversing with teachers on student violent writing, 73–75, 77, 78
  disturbed by teacher responses to graphic writing, 3, 4
  follow-up conferences with assigned, 97
  "high-impact school leader," 36
  how they influence school culture, 34–36
  legal primer for, 11–29
  qualities required to improve school culture, 38

responding to student violent writing, 93–99

review of teacher classroom policies by, 75–76

staying informed on social and legal student expression issues, 68–69

suggesting teaching methods to teachers, 76–77

when off-campus writing targets a, 67–68

School administrators (K-6 schools)
applications for handling school violence, 8–9

applications on off-campus writing, 70

applications for promoting citizenship education, 27–28

applications for promoting creative writing, 61

applications related to school culture for, 39

applications for responding to violent writing, 98–99

applications for school policies, 48–49

applications for threat assessment, 89–90

School administrators (7–12 schools)
applications for handling school violence, 9

applications on off-campus writing, 70–71

applications for promoting citizenship education, 28–29

applications for promoting creative writing, 61–62

applications related to school culture for, 40

applications for responding to violent writing, 99

applications for school policies, 48–49

applications for threat assessment, 90–91

School boards, 35

School climate
establishing a positive, 37–38

qualities of a principal for improving, 38

School counselors
Lovell case on threat against, 86, 94

required student meetings with, 97

School culture
how schools are affected by the, 32

how student writing reflects on their, 32–34, 38

identifying the characteristics of a, 31–32

improving your, 37–38

practical applications for teachers and administrators on, 39–40

questions to consider on, 41

school administrator's influence on, 34–36

threat assessment guide on anecdotal writings about, 34

School Law Reporter (ELA monthly), 69

School newspaper *Hazelwood* decision, 16–18, 19, 20, 25, 26, 46

School policies
avoiding vague terms such as offensive or appalling in, 48

creating documentation trail as part of, 96

disciplinary options to consider, 96–97

examples of different, 46–47

incorporating legal principles into, 45–46, 47–48

practical applications for teachers and administrators, 48–50

on reasonable responses to all student violent writing, 95

on timely response to student violent writing, 93–95

zero tolerance approach, 43–45

School violence
a brief history of, 1–2

general indicators of trouble teen and potential, 54–55

how it has affected community or school, 9–10

preparing to work with outside-school, 9

school communication to parents about, 10

student violent writing as predictor of, 54–55

writing as substitute for, 55–56

See also Student violent writing; Threat assessment

Schools
citizenship education by, 21–24, 26–29

Cuff case on "wish to blow up" the, 33

cyberbullying prevention programs, 66–67

First Amendment rights issue for today's, 5–6, 12–13

freedom of expression in today's, 11–20, 24–29

legal primer for, 11–29
 student safety issue of, 32–40, 43–45
 true threat standard for assessing
   threatening speech, 20–21
 See also Case law; Disciplinary actions
Schoonover, B., 45
Schoonover, J., 44
Scott, R., 23
Shelton v. Tucker, 24
Sheras, P., 83, 89
Skiba, R. J., 35, 37, 44
Slongje, R., 66
Smith, P. K., 66
Socorro Independent School District,
   Ponce v., 94
Stakeholders, school communication
   about violence to, 10
Student arrest case, 7
Student expression
 Columbine effect on responses
   to, 5–10
 Fraser decision on vulgar or offensive,
   15–16, 19, 20, 24–25, 26, 46
 Hazelwood decision inconsistency with
   "basic educational mission,"
   16–18, 19, 20, 25, 26, 46
 legal primer for, 11–12
 Morse decision on illegal drug use
   promoted by, 18, 20, 25, 26, 46
 school policy regulating, 43–50
 staying informed on social and legal
   issues of, 68–69
 Tinker standard for assessing, 13–15,
   19–20, 24, 26, 46, 64, 65, 69
 true threat standard to assess
   threatening, 20–21
Student expulsion
 Columbine effect on First Amendment
   rights and, 5–6
 Gun-Free Schools Act (1994)
   mandating, 44
 zero tolerance policies on, 43–45
Student profiling, 83–84
Student safety
 bullying and, 32, 33
 how school administrator can
   influence feelings of, 34–36
 improving your school culture to
   improve, 37–38
 tips for improving school culture
   and, 39–40
 zero tolerance policy intentions for,
   43–45

Student suspension
 Bethel v. Fraser case on, 15–16, 19, 20,
   24–25, 26, 46, 65
 Charles Carithers for writing on chain
   saw, 6
 D.G. v. Tulsa on, 33, 93–94
 Kowalski decision on MySpace
   writing, 64
 Lovell v. Poway Unified School District
   on, 86, 94
 Matthew Parent for freewriting
   assignment, 7–8
 Ponce v. Socorro Independent School
   District on, 94
 timely response when taking action of,
   93–95
 zero tolerance policies on, 43–45
 See also Disciplinary actions
Student violent writing
 administration response to, 93–99
 applying legal cases to samples of,
   19–20
 the Columbine effect on responses to,
   5–6
 by the Columbine school shooters, 3–4
 common student emotions leading to,
   33
 cyberbullying, texting, and Facebook,
   66–67
 debate over Stephen King-like,
   57–58, 60
 eight-step threat analysis of, 85
 examples of student excuses presented
   in case law, 86
 freewriting, 52–54
 general indicators of potential violence
   in, 54–55
 importance of paying attention to
   warning signs of, 4
 by one of the Jonesboro shooter, 4
 keeping copy of all, 86–87
 media sources influencing, 51–52
 off-campus, 63–66
 as predictor of violence, 54–55
 principal-teacher conversations about,
   73–78
 problems with applying zero tolerance
   policy to, 44–45
 published case law reflecting school
   culture role in, 33
 school culture reflected in, 32–34
 school policy regulating response to,
   43–50

staying up to date on legal and social issues of, 68–69

when a teacher or administrator is target of, 67–68

See also School violence; Threat assessment

Student writers

Columbine effect on First Amendment rights of, 5–8

common student emotions leading to violent writings by, 33

eight-step threat analysis of, 85

Fraser decision on vulgar or offensive speech by, 15–16, 19, 20, 24–25, 26, 46

Hazelwood decision on speech inconsistent with "basic educational mission" by, 16–18, 19, 20, 25, 26, 46

journal writing by, 55–56, 59–60, 75, 76

Morse decision on speech that promotes illegal drug use, 18, 20, 25, 26, 46

newspaper and yearbook expression by, 16–18, 25

promoting illegal drug use, 18

rewriting assignments given to, 97

Tinker standard to assess expression by, 14–15, 19–20, 24, 26, 46, 65, 69

See also Violent student writing; Writing classroom

Students

citizenship education of, 21–25

Columbine effect on First Amendment rights of, 5–8

FBI list on traits of troubled youth, 54–55

survey (2003) on weapons carried by, 2

See also Disciplinary actions

Suicidal tendencies, 33

Teacher classroom policies

administration review of the, 75–76

on "confidentiality," 75, 76

principal-teacher communication on, 73–78

recognizing potential syllabus problems, 75

See also Writing classroom

Teachers

advice for all writing, 59–60

anger toward, 33

Columbine effect and practical applications for, 8–9

follow-up instruction as part of disciplinary action, 97

importance of paying attention to warning signs, 4

keeping copy of student writing, 86–87

positive responses to Columbine shooters' graphic writing by, 3, 4

principal conversations on student violent writing with, 73–75, 77, 78

principal teaching suggestions made to, 76–77

recognizing potential syllabus problems, 75

staying informed on social and legal student expression issues, 68–69

survey (2004) on support toward zero tolerance policy, 44

when off-campus writing targets a, 67–68

See also Writing classroom

Teachers (K-6 schools)

applications for handling school violence, 8–9

applications on off-campus writing, 70

applications for promoting citizenship education, 27–28

applications related to school culture for, 39

applications for responding to violent writing, 98–99

applications on school policies, 48–49

applications for threat assessment, 89–90

applications when teaching creative writing, 61

Teachers (7–12 schools)

applications for handling Columbine effect, 9

applications on off-campus writing, 70–71

applications for promoting citizenship education, 28–29

applications related to school culture for, 40

applications for responding to violent writing, 99

applications for school policies, 49–50

applications for threat assessment, 90–91

applications when teaching creative writing, 61–62

Texas A & M University shooting, 1
Threat assessment
    description of, 81, 82
    eight-step analysis of student writer
        and writing for, 85
    FBI's threat assessment model for,
        81–82, 84
    guide on anecdotal student violent
        writing, 34
    guide to manage school, 34
    as not being profiling, 83–84
    practical applications for teachers and
        administrators, 89–91
    Redfield's model on student writing
        used for, 82
    "Threat assessment in school" report
        (2002), 83
    Tinker standard used for, 14–15, 19–20,
        24, 26, 46, 64, 65, 69
    true threat standard for, 20–21
    two principles forming foundation
        of, 81
    See also School violence; Student
        violent writing
Threat Assessment Form for Student
        Violent Writing Incidents
    on information provided to law
        enforcement, 89
    on origination of writing, 87
    on questions for student author, 88
    on questions to ask parents or
        guardians, 88
    on teacher interview questions, 88
    on thematic issues within the
        writing, 88
"Threat assessment in schools: A guide
        to managing threatening situations
        and to creating safe school
        climates" report (2002), 83
Threat assessment strategies
    eight-step analysis of student
        writing, 85
    keep a copy of student writing,
        86–87
    listening and interacting with student,
        85–86
    Threat Assessment Form for Student
        Violent Writing Incidents, 87–89
    true threat test, 20–21
Tinker standard
    application to public schools, 26
    applied to two classroom writing
        samples, 19–20

case law decisions on MySpace parody
        page not meeting, 65
case law decisions on MySpace
        principal parody pages, 65
Kowalski decision application of
        MySpace threat and, 64
origins and description of, 14–15,
        24, 69
school policy consideration of the, 46
Tinker v. Des Moines Independent School
        District, 13–15, 24, 26, 46, 64, 65, 69
True threat test, 20–21
Tucker, Shelton v., 24
Tulsa, D.G. v., 33, 93–94

Uerling, D. F., 21
U.S. Constitution
    Civil Rights Act (1871), 12–13
    Fourteenth Amendment, 12, 14
    freedom of expression under the,
        11–20, 24–29
    U.S. Supreme Court given task to
        protect and interpret the, 25
    See also First Amendment
U.S. Department of Education
    guide for creating a "safe" school
        culture by, 36
    guide to manage threat assessment in
        schools by, 34
    school survey on student threat of
        physical attacks/bullying, 2
    "Threat assessment in schools: A guide
        to managing threatening
        situations and to creating safe
        school climates" report (2002)
        by, 83
U.S. President
    art class assignment threatening the, 7
    "perfect day" assignment threat
        against, 7
U.S. Secret Service
    guide for creating a "safe" school
        culture by, 36
    guide to manage threat assessment in
        schools by, 34
    indicators of trouble teen and potential
        violence, 54–55
    investigation of student violent
        writing by, 7
    Secret Service Investigates (2006), 7
    Secret Service Questions (2004), 7
    "Threat assessment in schools: A guide
        to managing threatening situations

and to creating safe school
climates" report (2002) by, 83
U.S. Supreme Court
    protector and interpreter of U.S.
        Constitution task of, 25
    recognition of school "mission"
        by the, 24–25, 26–27
    See also Case law
USA School Violence Statistics, 1

Valley Central School District,
    Cuff v., 33
Vietnam War protest case, 13–15, 24
Virginia Tech University shooting,
    1, 83
Vulgar student speech, 15–16

Washington Post, 5
"Well-Managed School" series, 23
West Virginia Board of Education v.
    Barnette, 11
Whitaker, T., 35, 73, 77
White, G. A., 93
Winter Olympics (2002) torch run
    banner, 18
WiseSkills, 23
Woodland R-IV School District,
    Beussink v., 33
Writing classroom

advice for all teachers on policies for,
    59–60
"Considering Purpose, Audience, and
    Tone" lesson in, 58–59
debate over Stephen King-like writing,
    57–58, 60
freewriting in, 52–54
indicators of violence in student
    writing, 54–55
practical applications for, 61–62
principal-teacher conversations about,
    73–78
recognizing potential syllabus
    problems for, 75
unique nature of the, 56–57
use of writing as substitute for
    violence in, 55–56
See also Student writers; Teacher
    classroom policies; Teachers
"Writing Our Stories" (antiviolence
    writing program), 55–56

Yearbook *Hazelwood* decision, 16–18, 19,
    20, 25, 26, 46

Zero tolerance policy
    description of, 43–44
    problems related to student violent
        writing, 44–45

CORWIN

A SAGE Company

The Corwin logo—a raven striding across an open book—represents the union of courage and learning. Corwin is committed to improving education for all learners by publishing books and other professional development resources for those serving the field of PreK–12 education. By providing practical, hands-on materials, Corwin continues to carry out the promise of its motto: **"Helping Educators Do Their Work Better."**